MARKING TIME, MAKING PLACE

An Essential Chronology of Blacks in New Orleans Since 1718

Edited by

James B. Borders IV

Beckham
Publications Group, Inc.

SILVER SPRING

Library of Congress Cataloging-in-Publication Data

Names: Borders, James B., IV.
Title: Marking time, making place : an essential chronology of Blacks in New
    Orleans since 1718 / edited by James B. Borders IV.
Description: Silver Spring, MD : Beckham Publications Group, Inc., 2015. |
    Series: James B. Borders IV Black history series | Includes
    bibliographical references and index.
Identifiers: LCCN 2015048750 (print) | LCCN 2015049089 (ebook) | ISBN
    9780982794340 (alk. paper) | ISBN 9780990590491 ()
Subjects: LCSH: African Americans--Louisiana--New
    Orleans--History--Chronology. | New Orleans (La.)--History--Chronology.
Classification: LCC F379.N59 N4326 2015 (print) | LCC F379.N59 (ebook) | DDC
    305.896/073076335--dc23
LC record available at http://lccn.loc.gov/2015048750

CONTENTS

I hope you like my work enough to like me on Facebook.
www.facebook.com/jb.borders

Please leave a review too on Amazon!
http://tinyurl.com/z9kjhyh

INTRODUCTION

Birthplace of jazz and gumbo. Home of Mardi Gras and Voodoo. Stronghold of Creoles, coons, buckjumpers and brass bands. Founded by the French, traded to the Spanish and sold to the Americans. Wealth created by indigo and timber, shipping and smuggling, then sugar cane, enslaved Africans, cotton trading, oil and gas exploration, tourism. That's New Orleans in a nutshell.

There is more to the place, of course. It doesn't seem particularly romantic or exotic to natives; it's merely home. In fact, it's hardscrabble for many. Struggle is non-stop, victory elusive. It's comfortable and comforting to many despite the heat, humidity, poverty and potholes. It's beautiful, elegant and endearing. It's also venal, shortsighted, ignorant, foolish and racist. It's a city both blessed and damned, haunted and hallowed, festive and morose: the Big Easy and the Big Sleazy, the City that Care Forgot and the Great Southern Babylon, the Mighty Resilient and the Weak Cliché, the Armpit of America and the Soul of the USA.

To its credit, New Orleans is also one of the most Africanized spaces in North America--culturally, spiritually and psychically. Moreover, as a robustly black space, there are and have been widely diverse and divergent expressions and gradations of the city's blackness--just like the hues of its people.

It's all here, it all fits, it all belongs, it's all blackness. Love it, hate it, don't give a damn. Nevertheless, as the late Haitian historian Michel-Rolph Trouillot once argued about his native land's past, the history of New Orleans also is filled with "moment(s) of retrospective significance" of which we all should be cognizant, especially as the city heads toward the 300th anniversary of its founding.

In order to appreciate this chronology more fully, here's some essential background information about how this fascinating repository of black life, this black mecca came to be.

Of course, it was never black folks' idea to create New Orleans; it just fell on us to build it and give it spirit. La Nouvelle-Orléans was founded in 1718 along the banks of the Mississippi (Mesachabe, "father of waters") River with the expectation that it would become the capital of France's Louisiana Territory, replacing Biloxi. That switch occurred in late 1721. It was named in honor of the Duke of Orléans, who was governing France on behalf of the boy king, Louis XV.

The site was selected by Jean-Baptiste le Moyne, Sieur de Bienville (commonly known as Bienville), the territorial governor who was also responsible for its development. The location was a piece of high ground surrounded by cypress swamps at a bend in the river near an old trail leading to a bayou (the natives called it Bayuk Tchoupik but the French would rename it Bayou St. Jean), that emptied into a large body of salt water, an estuary later to be named Lake Pontchartrain in honor of France's minister of finance. The locals often used the passageway as an entrance to the area when traveling from the east. It was preferable to trying to navigate the swift and treacherous currents of the big river. Ten years before the founding of New Orleans, Bienville had established a fort along the bayou near the lake. It was the river, however, that was far more important strategically to the French in their competition with the English and Spanish for control of North America.

In the first 12 years of its existence, New Orleans, like the rest of the Louisiana Territory, was managed by the Company of the West (Compagnie d'Occident, which later changed its name to the Mississippi Company and then the Company of the Indies), a publicly traded enterprise that had secured the exclusive 25-year right to extract wealth from the area. The public bought shares in the company believing that gold and other riches were just littering the grounds of Louisiana begging to be taken. When the gold didn't materialize, the Company's stock tanked in 1720. Its leaders persisted for another decade, however, trying to make the investment pay off.

An engineer, Adrien de Pauger, drafted the first plan for the town in 1722, encompassing what is now the Vieux Carré or French Quarter, consisting of 66 blocks. In these formative years, large plots of land on either side of the original city, and across the river from it, were given away to practically any white man willing to settle it. These early white settlers came from all parts of France as well as from Germany and Switzerland, displacing Choctaws and other Native American groups from their ancestral camping, hunting and fishing preserves.

From 1717-1719, French convicts had their sentences commuted and were forcibly shipped to Louisiana to help build the settlement in New Orleans. After three years of service, they were given their freedom and part of the lands they cleared. While many of those targeted for the program had been convicted of serious violent crimes, others were merely drunks, beggars and vagabonds. Nevertheless, deportation to Louisiana was generally regarded as a death sentence, given the heat, humidity, storms, mosquito and snake-infested swamps, communicable diseases and food shortages. So on January 1, 1720, at a prison harboring 107 French convicts destined for Louisiana, 50 of the inmates rioted, wounded two guards and escaped the facility. In May of that year, the king of France banned further forced deportations to Louisiana. By then, however, plan 1-A--bring on the Africans--was already underway. The native peoples were difficult to keep enslaved in their own lands. And, as one observer noted, though the soil was fertile, "it was soon discovered that European constitutions were not adapted to the burning suns of Louisiana, for they sickened and died." Africans, on the other hand, had already proven their adaptability to conditions in the New World. Maybe they could make the New Orleans gamble pay off.

THE ESSENTIAL CHRONOLOGY

1718 Among the first black people known to live in New Orleans are a couple of enslaved Africans named Jorgé and Marie. They belong to the city's founder and first governor, Bienville. Bienville will free Jorgé and Marie in 1735 or 1736 and their son Zacarie in 1743.

1719 *L'Aurore*, the first ship carrying enslaved Africans to Louisiana, arrives with a cargo of 200 captives on an unspecified date. There is no record of the names of those passengers. A second ship, *Le Duc du Maine*, brings a cargo of 250 to the French-controlled outpost at Biloxi the same year. Both ships, owned by the Company of the Indies, depart from the West African port of Whydah (also spelled Ouidah and Juda) in the nation that will become known as Benin in future centuries (and Dahomey before then, though the Dahomey Kingdom didn't conquer Whydah until 1727). During this period, Whydah is one of the most active slave-trading centers, exporting 15,000-20,000 enslaved individuals a year. It is an open port and slave ships flying French, English, Dutch and Portuguese flags all buy cargo there. A typical journey from West Africa to New Orleans takes 14 weeks on average but can range from 7 to 28 weeks, depending on a number of factors. Roughly 20 percent of the captives die along the way; others often die of diseases like scurvy shortly after landing. Before the arrival of *L'Aurore*, which means "the dawn," there were only "a handful" of enslaved blacks in New Orleans. A large swath of territory, later called the King's Plantation, is established on the West Bank of New Orleans at what will later be known as Algiers Point. Here the enslaved cargo is unloaded, penned up and allowed to rest and recover from the Atlantic crossing before being sold or assigned to other duties. Most of the Africans shipped to New Orleans during this period are members of the Bambara/Bamana ethnic group from the Senegambia region of West Africa. The captains of *L'Aurore* and *Le Duc du Maine* were charged specifically to bring Africans who were skilled cultivators of rice and barrels of rice as seed supply. (Okra, nkombo, may have been brought around the same time.) Over the long term, however, Africans from dozens of ethnic/ tribal groups and points of origin, including those born in the Americas, will find themselves in New Orleans, negotiating among each other and with white masters to either accommodate themselves to their status and condition or to resist and rebel against it.

A woman named Marie, who works as a domestic servant, and a man named Jean-Baptiste César, a laborer, are the first recorded free people of color to come to the city, though only one of them shows up in the first census taken two years later. One of the other free blacks in the city during its earliest years is Raphael Bernard. He appears in court records in 1724 to sue a white man for payment of a 200-livre loan Bernard had made to him.

1720 The so-called Mississippi Bubble (including investors in the development of New Orleans) bursts. The Company of the Indies, which has been granted the right to govern and manage the Louisiana territory on behalf of the King of France, sold shares in its operation to the public, promising investors an opportunity to profit handsomely. Led by a wealthy adventurer/rogue named John Law, the company's announced plan is to turn Louisiana into a profitable colony like Martinique and St. Domingue (later Haiti), which were founded decades earlier and have become major centers of sugar cane production. The plan for Louisiana was to make tobacco, rice and indigo principal crops to supply to the French in the same manner as Virginia tobacco and Carolina rice and indigo were being produced for consumption by the British. However, the early Louisiana tobacco crops are inferior, there are no instant riches to be had from gold or silver--as had been rumored--so investors lose confidence and the company's stock prices plummet. Conditions never improve markedly under their leadership and they will call it quits 11 years later.

1721 On April 20, the first cargo of enslaved Africans from Cabinde (Cabinda, in present-day Angola) arrives on *Le Nériède* with 294 captives.

On August 11, *Le Maréchal d'Estrées* arrives from stops in Saint-Louis and Gorée, Senegal, with a cargo of 196. Though "Louisiana" is the specified port of arrival, it is assumed that these enslaved were processed in New Orleans for the Company of the Indies, which owns the vessel.

The capital of the Louisiana colony is formally moved from Biloxi to New Orleans in December. The first census taken in New Orleans a month prior in November reports a population of 519 people: 171 enslaved Africans (33%), 1 Free Black (.02%), 21 enslaved Indians (4%), and 326 Whites (62.8%). Other reports of that first census peg the population at 470; in this tally, the white population is 277 (58.9%), the other figures are the same but their percentage of the population increases, e.g. enslaved Africans are 36% of the total population.

A hurricane hits the city for the first time since its founding, causing major flooding. Hurricanes will become a regular occurrence for the rest of the city's existence. Some will be more damaging than others. When the storms hit, invariably the black and the poor are among those who are most affected.

1722 Authorities for the Company of the Indies burn an unnamed enslaved African alive for killing a white man.

1723 *L'Expedition* arrives on some unspecified date (probably in the spring) from Gorée, Senegal, with a cargo of 91 enslaved Africans. An earlier stop in the voyage had deposited 7 captives at Biloxi.

Le Courrier de Bourbon deposits a cargo of 87 enslaved Africans at La Balise (Balize) on September 17. It is the French fort south of New Orleans at the mouth of the Mississippi River, current-day Pilottown in Plaquemines Parish. The Africans were purchased in Saint-Louis and Gorée, Senegal, and at a third stop in the Gambia. The ship's crew had to suppress an attempt by the enslaved to take over the vessel during the journey to New Orleans. This will be one of many such acts of resistance on the high seas, some successful, some not. The voyage left the African coast with 105 enslaved people. *Le Courrier*'s first stop across the Atlantic is Grenada, where three of the enslaved are offloaded. The 87 other survivors are then brought to Louisiana.

An enslaved man named Napi is the first person hanged to death in the Place d'Armes (present-day Jackson Square). He is convicted of killing his wife.

1724 The Black Code (Code Noir) is introduced and implemented in Louisiana and New Orleans by French authorities. It contains 54 articles detailing regulations about how the enslaved are to be treated and is based on a 1685 set of rules applied to French colonies in the Caribbean. Among other things, the Black Code forbids all marriages between white and black people in the Louisiana colony, regardless of status, and it mandates that the torture and killing of slaves be undertaken only by the government, not individual slave owners. The edict lays out specific punishments--like branding, ear cutting, leg crippling--that are to be administered to captured runaways. The Black Code also mandates that the enslaved be given one day of respite each week from their labors and that they be instructed in the Roman Catholic "creed," the only religion permitted. What the enslaved do with their time on these free days--Sundays and holidays--will do much to shape the culture of the entire city.

1725 New Orleans authorities hire a black man, Louis Congo (sometimes referred to as Jean-Louis Congo), to be its official punisher and executioner and watchman over the High or Bayou Road leading in and out of the city. (There is also a note in official records from 1720 that mentions a black man with a whip but no name is given for this individual.) Congo is reportedly freed from enslavement, given property along the Bayou Road, in what would later be considered Faubourg Tremé, and allowed to have his wife live with him. Congo's schedule of fees for providing his services is published--10 livres for a whipping or branding, 30 for a hanging, 40 for breaking a body on the wheel. It is presumed that he is permitted to do this work because Central Africans are a minority of the New Orleans population at this point and that Congo is competent in his work and likely literate as well. In 1726, three runaway Africans break into his home and try to kill him. In 1736, two other runaways jump him in broad daylight and beat him. Thereafter, Louis Congo vanishes from the city's written history.

....

1726 *L'Aurore*, owned by the Company of the Indies, returns on March 1 with a shipment of 290 enslaved Africans acquired in Saint-Louis, Senegal, for "Louisiana."

L'Annibal arrives at La Balise on an unspecified date with a cargo of 150 enslaved Africans acquired at Saint-Louis and Gorée, Senegal. Before reaching New Orleans, the ship makes a prior stop at Cap Francais in St. Domingue (Haiti), where it appears to have deposited as many as 176 captives.

John Mingo, a runaway from South Carolina, arrives in New Orleans naked and starving. A white man named Jonathas Darby takes him in, declares him free and permits him to live on a plot of land and to hire himself out for work. Mingo also agrees to purchase Thérèse from Darby in installments and to take her as his wife. However, four years later, when Mingo and Thérèse are managing enslaved people on another white man's plantation, Mingo will sue Darby for still claiming to own Thérèse even though the black man says she was paid for. The court cannot determine whether Mingo paid enough to complete the purchase, but it orders that the couple not be separated.

....

1727 The *Duc de Noailles* arrives on December 25, Christmas Day, at La Balise with a cargo of 262 enslaved Africans acquired at Saint-Louis and Gorée, Senegal. The ship had made a prior stop at Les Cayes, Saint-Domingue (present-day Haiti), where 18 captives were offloaded.

....

1728 On June 15, *La Vénus* brings a cargo of 341 enslaved Africans to La Balise. The cargo was acquired in the Senegambia region of West Africa.

La Diane arrives from the Bight of Benin on October 11 with a then-record 464 enslaved Africans (the voyage had started with 516 captives). They are offloaded at La Balise.

Antoine-Simon Le Page du Pratz (1695?-1775), a European settler in the Louisiana Territory, accepts a job as administrator of the plantation belonging to the Company of the Indies, which will become known as the King's Plantation in 1731. Located on the West Bank of the Mississippi, it is the place where enslaved Africans are disembarked and quarantined until they are either put to work on the plantation or sold to other local Europeans. Upon arrival at his new post, Le Page du Pratz makes the following observations: "The plantation looked like a forest half-cleared; the slaves' cabins were scattered about here and there. These blacks had several little pirogues that they used for crossing the river, to go steal from the habitants on the other side, where the town is. Every Sunday, at least four hundred slaves could be found on the plantation, of whom two hundred and fifty belonged there. I ordered the land cleared and cultivated. I broke up the slaves' pirogues and forbade them to ever have them again. I convened with the other settlers about what we had to do to prevent slave gatherings, which could only lead to trouble for the colony, and I succeeded in abolishing them." Le Page du Pratz will return to France in 1734; the enslaved will continue their weekly gatherings at other places on the outskirts of the city.

Le Page du Pratz also notes in his *The History of Louisiana*, which will be published in 1758, "A young slave who served the surgeon (on the King's Plantation) slept and lived in this last cabin, in order to do bleeding or apply first aid if a case was pressing. I learned several years later that this slave was one of the few good surgeons in the colony." This is the earliest mention of a black surgeon in New Orleans.

1729 *Le Duc de Bourbon* arrives at La Balise on October 16 with a cargo of 319 enslaved Africans acquired in Saint-Louis and Gorée, Senegal.

La Vénus returns to New Orleans on June 17 with 320 enslaved Africans purchased at Saint-Louis and Gorée, Senegal. The ship had stopped in Biloxi, where it seems to have offloaded up to 43 captives before docking in New Orleans.

L'Annibal leaves Senegal headed for New Orleans with a cargo of 300 but never makes it. A revolt by the Africans is beaten back by the ship's crew, which kills 45 of the enslaved and wounds an additional 47. The ship unloads the cargo in St. Domingue (Haiti) rather than risk the longer voyage to New Orleans.

Word reaches New Orleans in early December that an uprising by the Natchez Indians and several African allies has destroyed the Company of the Indies settlement at Natchez, 175 miles northwest of New Orleans. The French had selected the area as their tobacco-growing region and forced the Native Americans to be part of the undertaking's labor force. But when a new commander demands possession of the main Natchez village to annex to his own plantation, the natives stall the Frenchman until they can plan a counterattack. On the morning of November 29, they make their move and attack the French fort and other living quarters, killing 230 white men but sparing women and enslaved Africans. It is a major blow to the fortunes of the Company of the Indies. The French later wage a retaliatory campaign against the Natchez using Choctaw (aka Chahta or Chata) and African forces (an alliance they later regret fostering). The fighting will go on for several years, forcing the Natchez eventually to seek refuge among the Chickasaws, then the Creeks and, finally, the Cherokees before disappearing as a distinct people by the mid-1730s.

Simon Calfat and 14 other enslaved Africans are granted their freedom by Governor Étienne Périer, who took over from New Orleans founder Bienville in 1727, in exchange for massacring a peaceful settlement of Native Americans, called Chouchas, near New Orleans. The move is considered retaliation for the Natchez tribe using black allies to massacre 230 whites at Natchez weeks earlier. The attack on the Chouchas is also intended to drive a wedge between the natives and the Africans--to make them enemies, not allies. This becomes a standard tenet of early French colonial policy. The freedmen from New Orleans will later participate in other military expeditions with the French against the Natchez and Chickasaws, both of whom were more willing and capable of defending themselves than the Chouchas.

1730 *Le Saint Louis* arrives at La Balise on October 20 with a cargo of 180 enslaved Africans acquired at Saint-Louis and Gorée, Senegal. The ship, owned by the Company of the Indies, deposited 102 captives in Martinique and 45 at Les Cayes, Saint Domingue (Haiti) before heading for New Orleans.

1731 On June 24, Samba, an enslaved Bambara who had been the chief interpreter at the Company of the Indies plantation in Algiers, is tortured to death in the town square, Place d'Armes (current-day Jackson Square), along with seven other of his enslaved Bambara kinsmen. They had been accused of plotting a revolt involving as many as four hundred Bambara in and around New Orleans. Louis Congo, the black public executioner, not only tortures the eight men on the wheel, he also hangs an enslaved Bambara woman alleged to be part of the conspiracy. Samba is reported to have confessed to his role as leader of the revolt after authorities confronted him with evidence of his planning, along with admitting that they knew he was the same man who had worked as an interpreter at the principal French slave trading post on the Senegal

River, that he had led a revolt there that succeeded in ousting the Europeans temporarily and that when they later signed a treaty with the African rulers to resume their operations, one of the conditions was that Samba be sold into slavery in Louisiana, which he was, though not before attempting a revolt aboard ship during the passage. The woman hanged may be the same person who inadvertently alerts the French to the conspiracy. She is struck by a French soldier for refusing to obey an order he gave her. She responds by telling him that the French would not insult the enslaved much longer. The remark prompts an investigation that discovers Samba and his allies conducting a secret meeting at the Company of the Indies plantation.

The Company of the Indies collapses and Louisiana is returned to the French government as a crown colony. Instead of being a profit center for the French, Louisiana continues to be a money loser that requires larger and larger annual subsidies to stay afloat.

1736 On May 10, Charity Hospital is founded to care for the indigent of New Orleans thanks to a bequest from a French ship builder, Jean Louis, who had died in the city the previous year. Charity Hospital will become the nation's second oldest continually operating public hospital, after New York's Bellevue Hospital. Charity will undergo several changes in facilities, capacity and governance until its closing in 2005 after Hurricane Katrina. By then, it will have become a 2600-bed teaching hospital with the nation's number

#2 Level 1 Trauma Center and the major provider of medical care for most of the city's black poor. It will also have become a major employer of black health care workers and its closing will mean fewer jobs for working- and middle-class Afro-Orleanians to return to after the storm.

1743 *Le St. Ursin* brings a cargo of 190 enslaved Africans from Senegal, breaking a 13-year suspension of such shipments due to the uprising by Natchez Indians and a subsequent change in control of the Louisiana colony. However, no more enslaved Africans will be imported to the Louisiana colony again until 1758, when pirates and privateers begin smuggling enslaved people in noticeable numbers.

1751 The Regulations of Police, the first systematic code governing police conduct in the colony, goes into effect. It is prompted by a scandal in which the city's chief military and police officer is disciplined for profiting from the sale of alcohol to enslaved people. The new regulations also enforce white supremacy in the city by decreeing a punishment of 50 lashes and a hot-iron brand on any enslaved person who does not demonstrate "the respect and submission which he owes to white people."

1763 Louisiana is given to Spain by France as part of a peace treaty. With Spanish rule comes a policy called coartación, which permits enslaved people to buy their freedom for a "fair" price from their owners. Between 1769, when the Spanish actually settle in as rulers, and 1803, when New Orleans comes under the control of the United States, 1,330 enslaved New Orleanians purchase their freedom, despite having to sue owners in several cases to force them to uphold their end of the bargain. Additionally, another 166 enslaved people are freed by other blacks during this period, usually after having been purchased from white owners. Approximately 70 percent of these 1,496 manumitted people are female. As a result of all these "freedom purchases," the free population mushrooms from 99 at the beginning of Spanish rule to 1,566 in 1805, when New Orleans is in the hands of the English-speaking United States. The number of enslaved people grows from 1,227 to 3,105 during the same period.

Though Spain is given Louisiana in 1763, it doesn't send anyone to govern the territory until 1766. The local leadership, still loyal to France, revolts against the change in ownership and, in 1768, sends the first Spanish governor, Antonio Ulloa, back to Havana, Spain's major outpost in the Americas. The following year, Alejandro O'Reilly, is sent in to govern and to put down the revolt. He does so with a force of 2,056 soldiers from Cuba, 160 of whom are free black militiamen--80 from the pardo (light-skinned and mixed race) unit and 80 from the moreno (dark-skinned and pure black) unit. Most of these soldiers will return to Cuba in 1770 when O'Reilly's appointment as governor ends.

1766 The French-owned King's Plantation closes. Among its inventory are 241 enslaved people. Opened at the founding of New Orleans on the west bank of the Mississippi River, the property was used to quarantine enslaved Africans upon arrival and to prepare them for sale or work on the plantation. Over time, the plantation expanded for miles along and behind the river front. Enslaved people cleared the land, planted crops and built structures. Some were also trained to be boatmen, lumber millers, carpenters and other skilled workers. White landowners were frequently sold enslaved people on credit by the King's Plantation during the period when the Company of the Indies had a monopoly on operations in Louisiana and later, when the place became a royal colony supported by subsidies from the French government. At the time of its closing, the King's Plantation is one of the largest labor camps in the region.

1769 The first census taken under Spanish rule tallies the population of New Orleans at 3,129: 1,227 Enslaved (39.2%), 99 Free People of Color (3.2%) and 1,803 Whites (57.6%).

1770 Between 1770 and 1810, white slave-owners in New Orleans will emancipate 1,258 enslaved people free of charge for no stated reason, for "long and faithful service" or simply out of "love and tenderness."

1771 The Spanish crown issues royal orders encouraging the importation of enslaved Africans to Louisiana. The orders will be renewed annually through 1780.

In 1777, Spanish slavers will be permitted to import enslaved people from the French Caribbean. In 1782, enslaved people will be allowed to be imported duty-free. In 1786, however, the Spanish will begin restricting the trade, finally banning it outright in 1796. The ban will last four years.

Plantation owner Juan Baptiste Cézaire LeBreton, a former musketeer in the French Royal Army, is shot to death at his labor camp in what later became the Carrollton section of the city. Spanish officials use torture to extract a confession out of the enslaved people belonging to LeBreton. The guilty party has his head and hands cut off. Other enslaved Africans implicated in the killing receive 200 lashes and have their ears cut off.

1772 Marie-Jeanne, a woman of color, is manumitted in New Orleans on December 5. She takes the last name of her wealthy white lover, Francois Lemelle, and a decade later leaves the city to settle near Opelousas, LA, on 800 acres of land given to her by Lemelle, who had moved to the area around the time she was freed. Marie-Jeanne Lemelle, her five sons and 15 slaves given to her by Francois Lemelle make improvements to the land. Then the mother divides her holdings among the five sons, making them men of property and, therefore, prestige.

1778 The Code of 1778 issued under Spanish rule updates the Black Code of 1724 that the French imposed. The new laws contain 72 articles, up from 54 in the original, and have been written to serve the interests of slave-owners. Among other edicts, it "entirely forbid(s) assemblies held by Negroes in observance of the deaths of their fellow [enslaveds]" and that any white person who marries a black be driven out of Louisiana. The Code will receive another major update in 1808 when the Americans come to power.

1781 Marie Glass, a free woman of color who has been living along False River, just north of Baton Rouge, is executed in New Orleans on July 26 after being found guilty of torturing and killing her servant, a 15-year-old white girl, Emilia, whom witnesses (including Marie's mate, a white man named John Glass) say she routinely and viciously brutalized. After being found guilty, Glass's right hand is cut off and she is hanged. Her corpse is left on display "until the flesh fell off her bones." Then her head is severed, brought back to the site of her former home and placed on a pike as a warning to others.

1782 A detachment of 29 colored militia under the command of a white Spaniard, Captain Bautista Hugon, goes out from New Orleans in search of runaway enslaved Africans led Juan St. Malo (also Juan San Malo as well as Jean St. Malo in French records). St. Malo and company are reported to have made encampments in several locations around Lake Borne, east of the city. The four maroons guiding the militia lead them into an ambush, however. One of the soldiers is killed and several others are wounded. No runaways are captured during this campaign. The Spanish will return again the following year.

1783 Lt. Guido Dufossat of the Spanish colonial Fixed Infantry Regiment of Louisiana leads a contingent of black and "free mulattoes" militiamen to hunt down maroons along Lake Borne on the outskirts of New Orleans. The force kills one maroon and captures 23 others on March 1, 1783, in raids on two encampments, thanks to information provided by an ex-maroon named Chacala, whose reward is 200 pesos and freedom from enslavement. Once captured, some of the maroons tell everything they know about Juan St. Malo, the leader of the group, and the inner workings of the maroon settlements in the area. The following year, St. Malo, who had barely escaped the 1783 attack, will be captured.

The Perseverance Benevolent and Mutual Aid Association, thought to be the first black benevolent society in the nation, is founded in March to provide a safety net for its members during times of emergency. Perseverance Hall No. 4, built in 1819, will still be in existence in Louis Armstrong Park in the 21st century. It, like the halls of many other benevolent societies, will be used for political meetings and frequently will be rented out for social functions, balls, dances and recitals.

Spanish colonial records for New Orleans slave shipments are largely nonexistent but some researchers have calculated that between 1783 and

1796, 34 slave ships brought an estimated 8,500 enslaved people to New Orleans, mostly through ports in the Caribbean. An estimated 47 ships carrying 11,000 people are believed to have arrived in Louisiana altogether during this period.

1784 On June 19, maroon leader Juan St. Malo is hanged by Spanish authorities along with several of his comrades in what will later be known as Jackson Square. Their bodies are left out in the public square to rot. St. Malo was the leader of a band of runaway slaves captured days earlier after skirmishes near their stronghold in the cypress swamps of present-day eastern New Orleans. He will go on to be immortalized in a Creole folk song and will become the patron saint of runaway slaves. His origins will remain mysterious, as will his activities and the number of years he survived as an escapee from the D'Arensbourg plantation, north of New Orleans on the German Coast. Estimates of the number and size of the communities of maroons St. Malo led will range from the 60 captured along with the rebel leader (40 men, 20 women) to the 500 his key settlements, including one called Ville Gaillarde ("strong and sturdy town"), were reportedly built to accommodate. St. Malo's forces have been battling the Spanish authorities, aided by black informants, for at least two years and the Spanish colonial governor reports that 103 maroons had been captured altogether. In the attacks and skirmishes, several other runaways escape from the Lake Borne and eastern New Orleans area and circle back south, deeper into the swamps of Barataria Bay (later to become the stronghold of the pirate and slave smuggler Jean Lafitte) and are never conquered.

1786 Spanish colonial authorities, led by Governor Esteban Miró, decree that all women of color, free or enslaved, are required to wear "their hair bound in a kerchief" while in public and to refrain from "excessive attention to dress." The edict is intended to harden the colony's racial hierarchy. These head wraps are known as *tignons* in the local parlance and some black women subvert the order by making their *tignons* items of exquisite fabric, design and adornment. Nevertheless, restrictions on dress continue to tighten to the point that free blacks are not even permitted to copy the fashions of their white neighbors. As a result, however, black women become such skilled seamstresses and modistes that white women begin to seek out their services, especially for fancy ball gowns.

1788 The total New Orleans population is 5,319: 2,126 Enslaved (39.9%), 823 Free People of Color (15.5%) and 2,370 Whites (44.6%). This black majority will be maintained until the 1840 census.

On March 21, Good Friday, a huge fire breaks out in the Chartres Street home of Jose Nunez, the treasurer for the local Spanish government. The blaze quickly spreads and destroys 856 of the 1,100 structures in the small, compact city. There is no great loss of life during the catastrophe and, indeed, the Good Friday fire eventually becomes a good day for enslaved blacks in the city who will earn extra wages helping with the rebuilding effort. Some of these enslaved people will use these earnings to purchase their freedom or that of family members.

The *Catherine (Caterina) Santa Catalina* arrives at La Balise on September 9 with 204 enslaved Africans acquired from some unspecified location.

1789 James Durham (also Derham and Derum in some records) (1757-1802?), the first African American to formally practice medicine in the United States, returns to New Orleans and resumes his medical practice in the Crescent City. Durham had been born enslaved in Philadelphia. He had been taught to read and write and had been owned by a couple of prominent physicians, including George West, a surgeon for the British army who trained Durham to be a physician's assistant. After the American Revolutionary War, Durham was sold again and brought to New Orleans in 1783 to perform medical services for his owner, Dr. Robert Dow. Durham soon purchased his freedom for 500 pesos and established his own medical practice treating free people of color and the enslaved as well as whites. In 1788, he returned to Philadelphia for some reason and met Dr. Benjamin Rush, America's most prominent physician and medical scientist. When Durham returns to New Orleans, he launches a long-term correspondence with Rush. It is to Rush that Durham reports in 1800 of having successfully saved 53 of 64 patients he treated during a yellow fever outbreak. In 1801, however, Durham's practice will be restricted "to cure throat disease and no other" by Spanish authorities because he has no medical degree. In 1802, Durham disappears from the historical record and is never heard from again.

1792 The *Aimable Victoire* arrives on July 18 with a cargo of 307 enslaved Africans acquired in West Central Africa.

Dances in New Orleans are officially segregated by order of the Spanish colonial government.

1794 Another huge fire destroys 212 buildings in the city on December 8. As was the case after the Great Fire of 1788, all wooden buildings will be replaced by structures built in the Spanish style with thick brick walls. Wrought iron balconies will also become prominent. Black craftsmen will do much of this work.

1795 A planned interracial rebellion in Pointe Coupée, 100 miles north of New Orleans, is betrayed and quashed before it begins. Fifty-seven Africans and free people of color are executed for their participation in the conspiracy. Their decapitated heads are placed on poles along the road from Pointe Coupée to New Orleans. By this time, the Haitian Revolution is in full-combat mode and white rulers are fearful, paranoid even, that the struggle will spread.

1796 The Spanish government bans the importation of enslaved people to Louisiana. The *Virgen del Carmen* is the last ship to bring a cargo of enslaved Africans to the city in this y.ear.

The Carondelet Canal is formally named for the Spanish governor of the Louisiana territory (from 1791-1797) who ordered it built. Also known later as the Old Basin Canal, the 1.6-mile waterway built by black laborers in 1794 connects the city's French Quarter to Bayou St. Jean (which will be renamed Bayou St. John in later years) and expedites the shipment of goods to and from the city. (A New Basin Canal will be completed in 1838 in the Uptown section of the city using imported Irish workers, who die in droves from yellow fever during the eight-year construction process.) The Carondelet/Old Basin Canal, which will be in continuous operation through the 1920s before being filled in and covered over in 1938, will also fuel development of land around it for commercial and residential purposes. This area will come to be called Faubourg Tremé in a few years and will be home to many free people of color and their enslaved property.

1800 At the end of this year, Louisiana slave owners and traders convince Spanish authorities to again permit the trading in enslaved Africans, which had been banned in 1796.

1803 The United States government purchases the Louisiana territory from France for $15 million ($238.7 million in 2015 dollars). The transaction occurs less than two years after Spain gave the area back to France, its original European colonizer, in 1801. The French sell the property because they cannot properly defend it and they need money to fight the Haitian Revolution. The 827,000 square miles that the U.S. buys will eventually comprise all or parts of 15 new states and two Canadian provinces. At the time of the purchase, New Orleans is the most valuable asset in the deal. During the Louisiana Territory Period (1803-1810), however, more and more constraints are placed on black aspirations even as the territory begins transitioning to a democratic form of government. Enslaved people are no longer guaranteed the right to purchase their freedom, as 1,496 of them had done during the period of Spanish rule, 1763-1803. And free people of color are excluded from participation in political activities. The land of the free is proving to be a hollow phrase for most blacks in New Orleans as the city begins to develop into the young nation's largest marketplace for the sale of enslaved people. Moreover, as part of their defiance toward American rule, French-speaking blacks and whites cling to their language and cultural traditions more fiercely than ever. This will negatively impact the struggle for black unity in New Orleans as more English-speaking black folk become residents of the city in the decades ahead.

On September 6, the *Confiance* brings a cargo of 170 enslaved Africans acquired at Saint-Louis, Senegal. Prior to arriving in New Orleans, the ship deposits 34 captives in Martinique.

The *Africain* brings a cargo of 144 enslaved Africans from the Senegambia region to New Orleans on an unspecified date after unloading 103 captives in Havana.

....

1804 On April 24, the *Sarah* deposits a cargo of 210 enslaved Africans acquired in West Central Africa.

Over the next 60 years, until all slave traders are officially ordered to close up shop, New Orleans will develop into the nation's largest slave marketplace with an estimated 135,000 enslaved Africans sold in the city. That's more than 13% of the estimated 1 million enslaved people who were forced to migrate from the Upper South to the Deep South between 1808 and 1865. The hunger for enslaved workers is due to a confluence of factors: 1) the invention of the cotton gin in 1793 makes it easier to separate cotton fibers from the plant's seeds; 2) textile mills in New England use steam technology developed in 1785 to increase their capacity to produce cloth and other products from cotton for worldwide distribution; 3) steamboats start being produced in the U.S. in 1807 and increase the ability to move cargo up and down the Mississippi and other major American rivers; and 4) the Louisiana Purchase opens up millions of acres of cheap land that will be used for agricultural production. Fueling the growth of the New Orleans slave market is its proximity to the Mississippi River Delta region, which becomes prime cotton-growing country at a time when the demand for cotton is so large some planters become millionaires after harvesting only three successful crops. The intense demand for enslaved black labor in the area surrounding New Orleans forces prices in the city's markets up to three times higher than in Virginia, which will become the country's major slave-breeding region.

....

1805 The total population of New Orleans is 8,222, according
to the census conducted under United States control:
3,105 Enslaved (37.8%), 1,566 Free Colored (19%)
and 3,551 White (43.2%).

On November 29, the *Alexander* delivers a cargo of
179 enslaved Africans acquired on the Congo River.

Albert Tessier, a white man, begins renting a dance
hall where he hosts dances twice weekly for free
quadroon women and white men only. At these
events, white men are presumably introduced to
women who can become their mistresses through a
process of negotiation known as *placage* (placement).
The branding of such events becomes so popular that
by the 1830s there will be regular advertisements for
several of them in local newspapers, though it is likely
admission is not restricted to light-skinned black girls
and wealthy white men looking for long-term romance
across the color line. Nevertheless, the phenomenon
continues and goes so far that a building at 717
Orleans Street even becomes known as the Quadroon
Ballroom. It will later serve as the home of St. Mary's
Academy from 1881-1965. By then, the quadroon
balls will have become romanticized in American
and European media as part of the exotic, alluring,
fascinating culture of New Orleans. The reality, more
likely, is that during the mid-19th century, when
three-quarters of America's millionaires are members
of the planter class with holdings along the Lower
Mississippi River, having mistresses of color in bawdy
New Orleans is probably the same kind of status

symbol as private jets and yachts will be in the 21st century.

....

1806 A revision to the Black Code now stipulates that only enslaved people 30 years of age and older may be freed by their masters, provided they have exhibited "honest conduct" throughout their enslavement.

A new state law obliges free people to exhibit "special respect" to whites. They are subject to fines and imprisonment if they insult or strike white people and they are prohibited from thinking of themselves as equal to whites.

....

1807 Free black men are officially prohibited from entering the Louisiana Territory.

The *Ethiopian* arrives on February 2 with 140 enslaved Africans acquired in West Central Africa.

A ship named *George Clinton* arrives on November 14 somewhere in Louisiana (New Orleans is not specifically cited) with a cargo of 100 enslaved Africans acquired at Saint-Louis, Senegal.

The *Miriam* arrives on November 21 with a cargo of 100 enslaved Africans acquired on the Congo River.

....

1808 The United States bans the importation of slaves from Africa, effective January 1. For the next 50+ years, a vigorous domestic trade in slaves will develop between cities along the Eastern seaboard like Baltimore,

Maryland, and Charleston, South Carolina. Roughly half of the enslaved people shipped to New Orleans come via these routes; the other half are brought in by land and river, mainly the Mississippi. And despite the ban, enslaved Africans continue to be smuggled into South Louisiana and brought to market in New Orleans and its surrounding plantation communities. Cases brought against smugglers will be prosecuted in New Orleans courts until 1820.

1810 The population of New Orleans more than doubles over five years and stands at 17,242: 5,961 Enslaved (34.6%), 4,950 Free Colored (28.7%) and 6,331 White (36.7%). The large increase is due to the arrival in 1809-1810 of nearly 10,000 refugees from St. Domingue (Haiti) via Cuba in the wake of the Haitian Revolution (1791-1804). Refugees from St. Domingue fled to Cuba throughout the revolution and found safe harbor there. But when relations between Spain and France soured in 1808, after Napoleon invaded Spain, the St. Domingue refugees in Spanish-ruled Cuba were forced to flee. Since other refugees have also made their way to New Orleans in previous waves, when New Orleans was still a Spanish colony with a French-speaking population, New Orleans once again becomes a key target for escape and settlement. The U.S. government has to make an exception for slave-owning refugees to bring their human chattels with them but they do so. The new émigrés include almost equal numbers of whites, enslaved Africans, and free people of color, many of whom are biracial, even though Louisiana had formally prohibited free black men from entering its borders a couple of years earlier. The St. Domingue/Haitian refugees and their descendants will go on to make major contributions to New Orleans in all areas of industry and culture.

Faubourg Tremé is officially incorporated into the City of New Orleans when Claude Tremé sells a large tract of land to the City Corporation for $40,000 ($606,000 in 2015 dollars). Tremé, a hatmaker from Souvigny, France, had served five years in prison from 1787-1792 for the murder of an enslaved man named Alejo in a case of mistaken identity and white hubris. Tremé was walking down the streets of the French Quarter early one morning when he heard someone holler the equivalent of "Thief, thief, stop thief." Tremé saw a black man up ahead coming out of a residence and proceeding to walk down the street. He called out for the man to halt but the fellow ignored his demand. Tremé then pulled out his pistol and shot, fatally wounding the man he later learned was named Alejo and who was innocent and was the property of another white man. Unable to compensate Alejo's owner for the loss, Tremé was locked up. The case is one of a few in which a white man in New Orleans serves time in prison for killing a black, then or later. Tremé's fortunes changed dramatically, however, when he married Julie Moreau in 1793. Moreau was heir to huge land holdings that her ancestors had acquired and enlarged since the earliest days of European settlement in the area. Tremé, who had been hounded for non-payment of debts for several years before his imprisonment, began selling lots from the property he gained control of through marriage. Most of the land is sold off between 1798 and 1810. Known free people of color purchase 13 of the first 37 lots offered for sale. Free blacks have lived in the area since the founding of the city and some simply expand their holdings by buying Tremé's parcels. In 1810, the Frenchman sells the remainder of the huge estate to the City of New Orleans. He and his wife then move out of town. The neighborhood will continue to be named for Claude Tremé, however, and will later brand itself as the oldest black community in the United States.

A ship called the *Alerta*, whose voyage seems to have originated in Havana and which was planning to return there after acquiring 197 enslaved Africans at the notorious Badagry (in present-day Nigeria) slave port, is hijacked at sea by privateers and brought to New Orleans at some unspecified date in the second half of the year, where 152 of the enslaved are offloaded. Of the original cargo of 197, 14 were sold at sea to another vessel and the unaccounted 31 individuals who started the voyage are presumed dead.

1811 The largest revolt of enslaved people in North America begins on January 8, 36 miles upriver from New Orleans. For three days, up to 500 enslaved people liberate themselves, burning three plantations, picking up weapons, killing two white men, causing others to flee for their lives and marching along the River Road toward New Orleans. After travelling 25 miles toward their destination, the uprising is crushed near what later became Kenner, LA, by a military force, including an army detachment and two companies of militia sent from the city. Altogether, 84 enslaved people are killed in the uprising and its aftermath; another 20 escape and are never recaptured. Days later, 18 of the revolt's leaders, including Charles Deslondes, are arrested, tried and beheaded. Their decapitated heads are then placed on poles between La Place and New Orleans as a warning to others. Seven enslaved people from the area are later freed in recognition of their efforts to prevent the revolt. The local black militia--which has been in existence since the days of Spanish rule but has not been fully authorized by the U.S. government out of concern that it would offend certain parts of the white American community--nevertheless volunteers to help put down the uprising. They are rewarded the following year by being formally written into the state's militia act as the Battalion of Chosen Men of Color, or later, simply as the Battalion of Free Men of Color. Four companies of 64 men each are permitted to be activated at the governor's discretion. Each man in the battalion not only has to be free, he also has to be a tax-paying owner or son of an owner of property worth at least $30,000.

1812 Louisiana becomes the 18th state of the United States of America on April 30. It had been a long and complex political journey that began to accelerate on March 26, 1804, when the U.S. Congress, by a vote of 66 to 21, divided the lands acquired in the Louisiana Purchase into two parts: the Territory of Orleans (present-day Louisiana) and the District of Louisiana, later called the Missouri Territory. President Thomas Jefferson then appointed 27-year-old fellow Virginian William C.C. Claiborne as governor of the Territory of Orleans, and the process immediately began for admission into the Union.

1813 Dutreuil Barjon Sr. (1799-?), a free person of color who was born in Jérémie, St. Domingue, during the revolution that will lead to it becoming Haiti, moves to New Orleans where he will become a noted furniture maker. Barjon will apprentice for three years under another free black cabinetmaker, Jean Rousseau. By 1821, however, he will have a shop of his own--first at 245 Royal Street and later a larger space at 279 Royal--that offers "to the public a large assortment of furniture made in this city, and in the newest and most fashionable style," as he advertises in 1834. Barjon will transfer the business to his son, Dutreuil Barjon Jr. (1823-1870), in 1855. Curiously enough, a Dutreuil Barjon will be mentioned in an August 1854 newspaper article as the killer of another free man of color, Michel Honoré. Near the corner of Ursuline and Roman streets in Faubourg Tremé, Barjon will stab Honoré 13 times after Honoré reportedly misses him with a pistol shot. The two quarreled five months earlier at a popular ballroom, though the reason will never be disclosed in the press. Barjon does not appear to have been prosecuted for this killing and it's not clear from the newspaper accounts whether it was the son or father involved in the incident. However, in 1856, Dutreuil Barjon Sr. is believed to have moved with his mistress to France, ostensibly to escape people he owes. He had filed for relief from his creditors in 1843 and some historians think his financial problems continued into the 1850s. A few researchers, however, think the senior Barjon didn't actually leave New Orleans; he merely had this story spread around town, perhaps to make some people think he was out of reach. At any rate, Dutreuil Barjon Jr., who learned the furniture-making trade in his father's shop, will continue operating the business until 1867, the start of Reconstruction in New Orleans, a momentary era of increased freedom and opportunity for black people, though not for wealthy whites who could afford fancy custom-made furniture. Pieces of furniture attributed to the Barjons would become collectors' items in the 21st century.

1815 The heaviest fighting in the Battle of New Orleans takes place January 8 on the outskirts of the city (in present-day Chalmette) when a mixed group of 4,500 local volunteers and the United States Seventh Infantry Regiment, under the command of General Andrew Jackson, repel and decimate a force of 8,000+ British soldiers attempting to take the city. The combatants on both sides are unaware that the War of 1812, which began six weeks after Louisiana was granted statehood, has ended with a treaty signed on December 24, 1814. Free and enslaved blacks fight on the side of the U.S. despite the fact that the British had offered emancipation to all enslaved people who made it to their lines. Approximately 2,400 enslaved black people throughout the South take advantage of this offer, but none apparently from New Orleans. Instead, the battle is remembered in the black community for the roles 600 black fighters play in serving the U.S. cause. They are led by a black veteran of the French army, Major Joseph Savary, who had fought against the armies of the enslaved in the Haitian Revolution and then fled the country in 1809 when the great wave of refugees from Haiti made its way to New Orleans. The black troops under Savary's command play a decisive role in the battle when they take the initiative to engage the enemy and one of their number shoots and kills the British commander, General Edward Pakenham, on the field of battle, leading to a rout of the British forces. The British suffer 2,000 casualties, the Americans 71. Despite receiving public praise from General Jackson for their valiant efforts in the battle, when the fighting ends and the British finally withdraw from Louisiana ten days later, Jackson asks all the black troops to leave the city. Local white citizens are reportedly concerned that the presence of armed blacks in New Orleans--and perhaps the memory of the 1,000 black West Indians fighting as free men on the British side--will instigate rebellions among the enslaved. Offended by the order, Savary and several of his followers leave town and make their way to Texas, where they fight for Mexico in its war of independence from Spain (1810-1821) under the leadership of the Afro-Indio-Mexicano revolutionary General Vicente Guerrero. By 1822, however, Savary will return to New Orleans. Nevertheless, the black veterans of the Battle of New Orleans never forget the insult to their honor.

With war over, peace and the increasing use of steamboats help the New Orleans riverfront grow into a powerhouse of economic activity until 1860. The waterfront will become a key place of employment for both skilled and unskilled black workers and the ancillary small black businesses, like food sellers, that support the waterfront workers and travelers to the city.

1817 The New Orleans City Council passes legislation on November 28 permitting and restricting enslaved people to gather on Sundays for dancing in Congo Square only, formalizing a practice that had been taking place since the earliest days of French rule and black presence in the area. Both free and enslaved blacks had gathered on these grounds outside the old city limits for commerce and recreation. The gatherings will continue until 1860, just prior to the onset of the Civil War and the occupation of New Orleans two years later by the Union Army. Congo Square will later be mythologized as the birthplace of truly American music and dance, the site where African, European and Native American cultural elements are fused into original expressions. Though benevolent societies and other black organizations will build several halls throughout the city that host dances featuring the bouncy music which will evolve into what comes to be called jass/jazz and despite the fact that other open air spaces like Lincoln and Johnson parks will become sites for weekly musical performances and band battles that more directly influence early jazz development, Congo Square will live on in local memory as the epicenter of black American culture, so much so that it will be added to the National Register of Historic Places in 1993 at the instigation of New Orleans residents. In 2011, the New Orleans City Council will officially change the site's name to Congo Square. In 1893, the space will be officially designated as Beauregard Square, named for a former Confederate general from neighboring St. Bernard Parish who will launch the first attack in the Civil War of 1861-1865. The popular name for the space will always remain Congo Square, however, even when large sections of it are replaced by the Municipal Auditorium, to be completed in 1929.

1818 A ship named *Josefa Segunda*, flying the Spanish flag, leaves Havana, Cuba, travels to the Bight of Biafra and the Gulf of Guinea to acquire 314 enslaved Africans. The vessel returns to Havana with 250 captives, unloads 18 of them, and sets sail for another destination in the Spanish empire (Florida? Mexico?) when it is intercepted by the U.S. Navy and brought to New Orleans on some unspecified date with 165 enslaved Africans. There is no accounting of the 67 individuals who are missing from the 232 captives aboard the ship when it left Havana and the 165 on it when the *Josefa Segunda* finally makes port in New Orleans.

1819 Over the course of this year, 1,348 enslaved people of African descent are brought by boat from other ports in the United States to be resold in New Orleans.

On August 4, Marie Laveau (1801-1881), a free woman of color, marries Jacques Paris, a free man of color who immigrated to New Orleans from Haiti. Paris will die--or disappear--the following year and Laveau will become the paramour/woman/wife of Louis Christophe de Glapion, with whom she will reportedly bear 15 children before his death in 1855--though records only verify five offspring. Laveau will become popularly known as a Voodoo priestess and one of her daughters, also named Marie (1827-1895), will carry on the role after the mother's passing. In death, their legend will grow and they will still be venerated by some devotees in the 21st century, though denounced by others as charlatans, hustlers and perverters of the true New Orleans Voodoo religion.

1820 New Orleans is home to 27,176 people, according to the census: 7,335 Enslaved (27.1%), 4,950 Free Colored (23%); and 13,584 White (49.9%). After achieving statehood, increasing numbers of English-speaking American whites begin settling in the city and creating a cultural divide between themselves and the French/Spanish/Haitian cultural mélange that formed in New Orleans before their arrival. The Trans-Atlantic Slave Trade Database will document 107,000 enslaved Africans who were brought to Louisiana between 1719 and 1820. Of those brought to New Orleans whose regional origin is identified, 37% are Central Africans (principally Angolan and Congo), 22% Senegambians (Mandingo, Bambara, Wolof), 15% from Benin (Dahomey), 14% Sierra Leone, 9% Biafra, with the remaining 3% split between Mozambique on the East

Coast of Africa and Gold Ghost (Ghana) on the West Coast.

Over the course of this year, 604 enslaved people of African descent are brought by boat from other ports in the United States to be resold in New Orleans.

Free people of color are permitted to buy season subscriptions to the French opera, Théâtre d'Orléans in the Vieux Carré, and to sit in a segregated section for 50 dollars; white patrons pay 60 dollars. The first opera was performed in the city in 1796 but the opera houses remained financially shaky, so it makes good business sense to reach as broad a range of customers as possible. The musicians performing at the opera are predominantly European immigrants but free people of color are also included. The opera house preferred by the English-speaking Americans in the city is the St. Charles Theater, on the uptown side of Canal Street. It, too, offers segregated seating for free blacks. These segregated seating policies at the opera will continue until the mid-1960s.

The New Orleans Independent Rifle Company advertises for "two young men of color" to be taught to play keyed bugles. Instruments, uniforms and a salary would also be provided.

1821   Over the course of this year, 2,746 enslaved people of African descent are brought by boat from other ports in the United States to be resold in New Orleans.

1822 Over the course of this year, 5,242 enslaved people of African descent are brought by boat from other ports in the United States to be resold in New Orleans.

1823 Over the course of this year, 1,413 enslaved people of African descent are brought by boat from other ports in the United States to be resold in New Orleans.

1824 Over the course of this year, 659 enslaved people of African descent are brought by boat from other ports in the United States to be resold in New Orleans.

1825 The first school for free children of color opens in the Tremé section of the city on a block of land purchased by Marie Aliquot, a French woman who will devote her time and fortune to help black people after being rescued from an "unpleasant incident" by an enslaved man. Aliquot will sell the land in 1836 to the Ursuline nuns on the condition that they continue to operate a school there for black children. The Ursulines will do so until 1838, when they will donate a portion of the land as the site for St. Augustine Roman Catholic Church, which will be built by black laborers and serve free and enslaved parishioners.

Over the course of this year, 1,668 enslaved people of African descent are brought by boat from other ports in the United States to be resold in New Orleans.

1826 Over the course of this year, 1,108 enslaved people of African descent are brought by boat from other ports in the United States to be resold in New Orleans.

1827 On November 20, Edmond Dédé (1827-1903), who will go on to become a violin prodigy and a noted composer and conductor in France, is born in New Orleans to free parents who migrated to the city in 1809 as part of the large contingent of former St. Domingue residents who had taken refuge in Cuba during the Haitian Revolution. Dédé will leave New Orleans in 1852, a time when restrictions are increasing on free blacks. He will eventually carve out a distinguished career in France and will return to New Orleans only once, for a brief period in 1893. Dédé is one of the earliest and most accomplished of several French-speaking New Orleans-born composers and performers who will make marks in the world of European classical music during the 19th century.

Over the course of this year, 1,359 enslaved people of African descent are brought by boat from other ports in the United States to be resold in New Orleans.

1828 Over the course of this year, 5,781 enslaved people of African descent are brought by boat from other ports in the United States to be resold in New Orleans.

1829 Over the course of this year, 2,931 enslaved people of African descent are brought by boat from other ports in the United States to be resold in New Orleans.

1830 New Orleans grows to 46,085 residents, according to the census: 14,476 Enslaved (31.4%), 11,562 Free Colored (25.1%) and 20,047 White (43.5%). The census also tallies 962 Free Colored slave owners in Louisiana, 751 of them living in New Orleans, or roughly 41% of the 1,834 heads of households counted among the Free Colored population.

Over the course of this year, 1,773 enslaved people of African descent are brought by boat from other ports in the United States to be resold in New Orleans.

A new state law requires all freed people to leave the state within 30 days of being granted their freedom unless they are granted a formal exemption to remain in Louisiana.

The Negro Philharmonic Society is founded. At one point, the orchestra reportedly will have more than 100 performers, including a few white members. The Society's director, Jacques Constantin Deburgue (1800-1861), is a black violinist and music teacher. Charles-Richard Lambert (?-1862) is the orchestra's conductor and the father of two musician sons, performer/composers Charles-Lucien Lambert Sr. (1828-1896) and Sidney Lambert (1838-1905) who will go on to have distinguished careers. The Negro Philharmonic Society will present performances of its own and presentations by visiting artists. Some of its members will also play regularly at the Theatre de la Renaissance, a venue for the free colored community. Racial hostility will put an end to the Negro Philharmonic Society prior to the Civil War but some of its former members, including musical prodigy Edmond Dédé and the Lamberts, will flee New

Orleans in the 1850s and enjoy successful careers in France and Brazil.

....

1831 Julien Hudson (1811-1844), a mixed-race free black, becomes the first-known person of color to be a professional painter in the South when he begins advertising his services as a miniaturist. The son of an English father and a mother who was a New Orleans free woman of color, Hudson apprenticed as a tailor before turning to painting in 1826. After furthering his studies in Paris in 1830 and 1831, he returns to New Orleans and sets up a studio in his mother's house in the French Quarter. He will die mysteriously at 33; a hushed suicide, according to some accounts. Specializing in portraits, only four of Hudson's signed paintings survive to the 21st century; one of them is a self-portrait.

The Louisiana Colonization Society helps a small group of free people of color in the state move to Liberia. Between 1831 and 1860, 309 free and freed blacks from Louisiana will repatriate to the African nation.

Over the course of this year, 3,082 enslaved Africans are brought by boat from other ports in the United States to be resold in New Orleans.

....

1832 Over the course of this year, 1,342 enslaved Africans are brought by boat from other ports in the United States to be resold in New Orleans. Among these numbers are six enslaved Africans ranging in age from 7 to 25 who arrive from Charleston, South Carolina, on September 3 aboard the schooner *Wild Cat*. A 7-year-old girl in the group is described as a mulatto; the only other female listed is 20 and is described as a Negro. So are all men in the group. One could speculate that the little mulatto girl was the daughter of the 20-year-old, which would have meant that she was 13 when she gave birth. The fact that the woman was demonstrably fertile would have enhanced her value on the auction block.

1833 Over the course of this year, 761 enslaved Africans are brought by boat from other ports in the United States to be resold in New Orleans.

1834 The Artisans Benelovent and Mutual Aid Society (La Société des Artisans) is founded as a literary organization and support network for workers and craftsmen. New Orleans blacks will go on to found hundreds of clubs, societies and organizations that bring people together in groups based on occupation, class, caste, religion and philanthropic purposes. Well into the 20th century, the black community in New Orleans will come to be regarded as one of the most organized in the country.

Over the course of this year, 921 enslaved Africans are brought by boat from other ports in the United States to be resold in New Orleans.

A fire breaks out on April 10 at the three-story Royal Street mansion of a white family headed by Leonard and Delphine LaLaurie. When police and firemen get there, they find an old enslaved woman chained to the kitchen and seven other enslaved people chained in the attic. All of them appear to have been tortured and imprisoned for a long period. In fact, complaints about Delphine LaLaurie's treatment of her slaves have been raised since 1831, including the death of a 12-year-old girl who fell/jumped off the roof to her death attempting to avoid a beating. The cook later will claim that she set the 1834 fire on purpose and was trying to kill herself rather than continue enduring the torture being inflicted on her. After the incident, a mob ransacks the LaLaurie mansion for more evidence of evil-doing, forcing the family to flee eventually to Paris.

1835 The Creole Wild West, the oldest Black Masking/ Mardi Gras Indian gang, is chartered in the State of Louisiana, according to assertions by the organization's current-day leaders. The Mardi Gras/ Black Indian masking tradition in New Orleans had been observed as early as 1732. Blacks masked then and continue to parade as Native Americans ostensibly as homage to the history of shared resistance to white supremacy. The masking Indians will acquire a reputation for violence, however, both toward outsiders and among themselves, that will take a long time to fade away. Nevertheless, by the 1960s, their syncopated call-and-response chants will make their way into New Orleans rhythm & blues recordings and by the 1970s, the Mardi Gras/Black Indians will begin securing acclaim for making increasingly colorful and elaborate costumes (suits) to parade in.

Over the course of this year, 4,723 enslaved Africans are brought by boat from other ports in the United States to be resold in New Orleans.

1836 The Economy Society (La Société d'Economie et d'Assistance Mutuelle) is founded. It will later be deemed "the most exclusive black organization in America" by one historian and other clubs will spring up to emulate its social policies. The organization becomes a club for the city's oldest and wealthiest French-speaking free people of color. In 1870, its members organize the Economy Hotel Joint-Stock Company, one of the more successful ventures of its type. However, the Economy Society is remembered today chiefly for its intra-group discrimination based primarily on skin color and its hall at 1422 Ursulines Street, a popular venue for early jazz performances.

Florville Foy (1819-1903) first advertises his services as a marble cutter. He will be said to have become wealthy from his work building monuments, grave stones and elaborately carved burial tombs for cemeteries in New Orleans and as far away as Pensacola, Florida. Foy establishes his studio on North Rampart. At its height, it will employ nine additional artisans. Florville Foy was the son of a French marble cutter, sculptor and writer named Prosper Foy who immigrated to New Orleans and took up with Heloise Aubry, a free woman of color. Together they had five children but only Florville survived. Florville's life partner is Louisa Whitaker, a white woman from Mississippi who will come to live with him in New Orleans in 1850. They will marry in 1885, during a brief period after the Civil War when interracial marriages will no longer be outlawed.

Over the course of this year, 3,056 enslaved Africans are brought by boat from other ports in the United States to be resold in New Orleans.

1837 Over the course of this year, 66 enslaved Africans are brought by boat from other ports in the United States to be resold in New Orleans.

The lifeless body of notorious maroon Bras Coupé is dumped in the Place d'Armes (present-day Jackson Square) where it remains for days while the city's enslaved population is forced to view the corpse. Once a tall, well-known dancer at Congo Square who was called Squire before losing his arm in a shooting incident, Bras Coupé had a $2,000 reward on his head when he was clubbed to death in a swamp outside the city. The runaway had been used as a bargaining chip in a publicity campaign by local police who were resisting efforts to disarm them due to their excessive brutality. The police claim they need their guns to save the city from violent criminals like Bras Coupé and his band of marauders. After stoking the fears of the white community, the police get their way and a manhunt for the maroon leader begins. He is shot on April 6 by bounty hunters but manages to elude capture. Fisherman Francisco Garcia later gives him refuge before deciding to bludgeon the wounded man to death and claim the reward for himself. After a great deal of haggling, Garcia is eventually paid $250 for his troubles.

1838 There are now so many brass bands parading city streets that The New Orleans *Picayune* describes it as "a real mania for horn and trumpet playing."

Over the course of this year, 1,669 enslaved Africans are brought by boat from other ports in the United States to be resold in New Orleans.

1839 Over the course of this year, 1,088 enslaved Africans are brought by boat from other ports in the United States to be resold in New Orleans.

1840 The population of New Orleans stands at 83,977, according to census figures: 18,208 Enslaved (21.6%), 15,072 Free Colored (18%) and 50,697 White (60.4%). The white population has increased by 150% in 10 years as cotton production has become a key driver of the American economy. New Orleans is now the largest city in the South and the fourth largest in the United States. This will be its highest ranking ever among the largest American cities.

Over the course of this year, 1,124 enslaved Africans are brought by boat from other ports in the United States to be resold in New Orleans.

On March 15, Jules Lion (1809-1866), a mixed-race native of France who had originally settled in New Orleans in 1836 or early 1837, mounts an exhibition of daguerreotypes, a forerunner of photographs, at the St. Charles Museum. It is the first exhibition of daguerreotypes in New Orleans and only the second in the United States. The revolutionary image-making process had only recently been invented in France by Louis Daguerre. Lion captures street scenes of New Orleans initially with his daguerreotypes and then turns his attention to portraiture. He has been trained initially as skilled lithographer, a style of printing invented in Germany in 1796, and will eventually return to that craft in the 1840s. More than 200 of his lithographs made between 1837 and 1847 will survive to the 21st century, including those that were initially made as daguerreotypes, none of which are known to still exist.

....

1841 Over the course of this year, 1,397 enslaved people of African descent are brought by boat from other ports in the United States to be resold in New Orleans.

....

1842 In September, construction of St. Augustine Roman Catholic Church, located in Faubourg Tremé at the corner of Bayou Road (present-day Gov. Nicholls Street) and St. Claude Street (which will become Henriette Delille Street), is completed. The land for the church was donated by the Ursuline nuns with the condition that the church be named in honor of their patron saint, St. Augustine of Hippo, the fourth century African bishop and theologian. Half the pews in the church are rented to free people of color; the side aisles are reserved for enslaved people.

The Sisters of the Holy Family (Soeurs de Sainte-Famille), a Catholic religious order for free women of color, is officially organized on November 21. It is founded by native New Orleanian Henriette Delille (1812-1862) along with another free black, Juliet Gaudin (1808-1888)--born in Cuba to St. Domingue/ Haitian parents who made the great migration to New Orleans in 1809, where her father opened a school for free children of color--and Marie Aliquot, a Frenchwoman who founded the first school for free children of color in New Orleans in 1825. In 1843, Josephine Charles (1812-1885), another free woman of color, will join the order. The group is created to nurse the sick, care for the poor and instruct the igno-rant. They initially organized in 1836 as the Sisters of the Presentation and for decades will have to overcome skepticism by church authorities that black women could lead celibate, spiritual lives. In 1847, a group of free blacks will form the Society of the Holy Family to provide financial and moral support to the order. In 1852, Delille, Gaudin and Charles will pronounce their first vows toward nunhood at St. Augustine Roman Catholic Church in Faubourg Tremé but will not be allowed to wear the black habits of full-fledged nuns until 1872. The work of the Sisters of the Holy Family will eventually expand to other parts of the United States as well as to Central America and West Africa. Among the long-standing institutions in New Orleans that they found are St. Mary's Academy and the (Thomy) Lafon Nursing Home (Lafon was a major financial supporter), on a 123-acre tract in eastern New Orleans that the organization will buy in 1906 for $10 an acre. The Sisters of the Holy Family will also build the St. John Berchmans' Orphanage with Lafon's support in 1892. In 1988, proceedings will begin to have Henriette Delille declared a saint in the Roman Catholic Church.

Over the course of this year, 924 enslaved people of African descent are brought by boat from other ports in the United States to be resold in New Orleans.

1843 On December 10, Norbert Rillieux (1806-1894) patents a method for refining sugar into crystallized granules that revolutionizes the sugar-making industry. In Rillieux's process, sugarcane juice is evaporated in a series of vacuum pans that heat one another in sequence, thus controlling the overall temperature and producing the desired crystallized form. This evaporation process is still used for producing freeze-dried food, pigments, and other industrial products. Rillieux was born in New Orleans to a white planter/engineer father, Vincent Rillieux, and a free woman of color, Constance Vivant, he could not marry at the time. Norbert, the oldest of seven children produced by this union, attended L'École Centrale engineering school in Paris, where he not only excelled, he also became the school's youngest faculty member in 1830, at age 24, when he began teaching applied mechanics there. He returned to

Louisiana in 1833 to serve as head engineer at a sugar refinery that is under construction but which will never be completed due to disagreements among the partners, who include Rillieux's family members and others. Nevertheless, Rillieux began working in 1834 on his process to improve the sugar refining process, which, at that time, had been highly wasteful and not very successful in extracting the liquid out of the sugarcane juice. After installing his sugar-refining process at a couple of major plantations in the New Orleans area, Rillieux will returns to France in the late 1850s and die in Paris on October 8, 1894.

Poet/teacher Armand Lanusse (1812-1867) publishes *L'Album Littéraire, Journal des Jeunes Gens, Amateurs de la Littérature* (The Literary Album, A Journal for Young People and Lovers of Literature).

Over the course of this year, 2,437 enslaved people of African descent are brought by boat from other ports in the United States to be resold in New Orleans.

....

1844 Dieu Nous Protège (God Protect Us) is founded. Its sole purpose is to buy and free enslaved people. Enslaved people bought and freed by the organization are then required to join the society and contribute funds to free others.

Over the course of this year, 1,464 enslaved people of African descent are brought by boat from other ports in the United States to be resold in New Orleans.

1845 *Les Cenelles* (The Holly Berries), an anthology of poems written in French by free men of color from New Orleans, is published. The 85 works in the volume are written by 17 poets. *Les Cenelles* is the first anthology of black writers in the United States. Armand Lanusse serves as the volume's editor. He will also serve later as the principal of the Catholic School for Indigent Orphans (L'École Des Orphelins Indigents) from 1852-1866. The school will be a hub for the city's black French-speaking artists, intellectuals, activists and philanthropists.

Over the course of this year, 3,002 enslaved people of African descent are brought by boat from other ports in the United States to be resold in New Orleans.

1846 Over the course of this year, 3,309 enslaved people of African descent are brought by boat from other ports in the United States to be resold in New Orleans.

1847 Over the course of this year, 2,774 enslaved people of African descent are brought by boat from other ports in the United States to be resold in New Orleans.

1848 The Catholic School for Indigent Orphans (L'École Des Orphelins Indigents) opens as the first school in the country to offer free education to African-American children. Madame Bernard (Marie Justine Cinaire) Couvent (c. 1757-1837), a freed woman born in Africa and widow of a prosperous black businessman, had bequeathed the land (at present-day 1941 Dauphine Street in the Faubourg Marigny section of the city) and money to build the school in her will. The school's first principal is Felicie Cailloux, wife of future Civil War hero André Cailloux. The school's structure, completed in 1852, will be destroyed by the so-called Great Hurricane of 1915. Sister Katherine Drexel, who opened Xavier University Preparatory School that same year, will agree to rebuild the school in exchange for control of its operation. It will be renamed Holy Redeemer School until it closes in 1993 and reopens as Bishop Perry Middle School for boys. When the Perry School is forced to close in 2006, the facility will be repurposed as the St. Gerard Majella Alternative School, designed to provide ongoing education to young women of high school age who are pregnant.

On October 6, the African Methodist Episcopal (AME) Church is issued a charter permitting it to operate legally in the state of Louisiana, even though the church opposes slavery and permits enslaved people to attend its services. A group of 10 incorporators will spearhead a collective effort to construct a new church structure at 222 North Roman Street and name it St. James Chapel AME Church. The Neo-Gothic structure will be added to the National Register of Historic Places in 1982. Before then, however, St. James will be known as an activist church that gets shut down by local authorities from 1858 until New Orleans is occupied by the Union Army in 1862. During the Civil War, St. James AME will serve as headquarters for a company of black Union soldiers. In the early 1960s, it will serve as the staging ground for boycotts and picketing of segregated Canal Street businesses.

Over the course of this year, 593 enslaved people of African descent are brought by boat from other ports in the United States to be resold in New Orleans.

....

1849 Over the course of this year, 2,117 enslaved people of African descent are brought by boat from other ports in the United States to be resold in New Orleans.

....

1850 The population of New Orleans rises to 116,368, according to the census. For the first time, the number of Enslaved declines from the previous census, from 18,208 to 17,011 (14.6% of the total population). The number of Free People of Color drops drastically to 9,905 (8.5%) from 15,072 in 1840. The White populace, however, continues its explosive growth, going from 50,697 in 1840 to 89,452 (76.9%). Some observers suggest that it is during this period that some blacks begin passing for white in significant numbers, though white officials will not start speaking out publicly about the matter until the 1870s, when some historians will claim that blacks in Louisiana began passing at a rate of 100-500 per year. The enslaved population in New Orleans drops during the 1840s because many slaveholders begin selling their urban slaves to rural plantations where the demand and price for enslaved people keeps rising. Most of the city-bound enslaved are deployed as domestics, porters and unskilled laborers, though some are also highly skilled and are hired out in the marketplace, usually at a profit to themselves and their owners.

Nearly 80% of the free people of color are literate by this point and over 1,000 of their children are attending school. And despite their relatively small numbers, free people of color in New Orleans are prosperous as a group, owning real estate valued at over $2.6 million ($74 million in 2015 dollars). Among their listed occupations are blacksmiths, clerks, copper smiths, jewelers, mariners, market men, medical doctors, ministers, moulders, musicians and music teachers, peddlers, painters, pilots, planters, sailmakers, ship carpenters, shoemakers, stevedores, stewards, tailors, teachers, upholsterers, laborers and a lithographer (Jules Lion, presumably). During the coming decade, however, more restrictions will be placed on the free black population. Though black New Orleanians dominate such trades as cabinet-making, carpentry, cigar manufacturing, masonry and plastering, they will be prohibited from owning certain businesses, including coffee houses and retail liquor outlets, and will be excluded from some professions, including river pilots and screwmen (the workers who tight-pack cargo on boats). Groups representing skilled white workers actively work to have free and enslaved blacks excluded from their ranks by law and practice. Free blacks also will be prohibited from fraternizing with enslaved blacks and, among other strictures, will be required to obtain formal permission from the mayor to become residents of the city.

Over the course of this year, 1,636 enslaved people of African descent are brought by boat from other ports in the United States to be resold in New Orleans.

1851 Over the course of this year, 1,623 enslaved people of African descent are brought by boat from other ports in the United States to be resold in New Orleans.

1852 Freed slaves in Louisiana are required to move to Liberia; this law will be repealed in 1855.

Over the course of this year, 1,579 enslaved people of African descent are brought by boat from other ports in the United States to be resold in New Orleans.

1853 The most deadly outbreak of yellow fever in New Orleans causes the deaths of 7,849 people, including many blacks, free and enslaved. There had been epidemics in previous years and there would be future outbreaks of the mosquito-borne disease--altogether between 1817 and 1905, 41,000 deaths will be recorded; the disease strikes annually with huge spikes of thousands of deaths every few years between 1819 and 1878--but none killed as many people as the "yellow jack" epidemic of 1853. Inventor Norbert Rillieux, who realized that mosquitos proliferated where there was standing water, devised a method for draining the swamps near the city but his proposal was quashed in the state Legislature by a business enemy of his father. Years later, a procedure strikingly similar to Rillieux's will be funded and successfully deployed. In the meantime, black nuns and nurses will care for the city's ill and many of the orphans yellow fever leaves behind.

Over the course of this year, 963 enslaved people of African descent are brought by boat from other ports in the United States to be resold in New Orleans.

1854 Over the course of this year, 573 enslaved people of African descent are brought by boat from other ports in the United States to be resold in New Orleans.

1855 The *Picayune* newspaper reports on January 19 that the police caught two white women living with William Jackson, who claims to be free. Police suspect he is a runaway and jail him until he can prove he is not. The two white women receive 50 lashes and 30 days in the workhouse. It is unusual for white women to be corporally punished for the crime of "amalgamation" with black men. In most of the other cases on record, the white women are fined and/or given up to six months in jail; the black men are whipped, fined and jailed, but unlike in the rest of the South, not lynched or castrated.

St. Luke's Episcopal Church is founded. It will become a pillar of the city's black Anglican community, including immigrants from Jamaica and other parts of the English-speaking Caribbean.

Over the course of this year, 604 enslaved people of African descent are brought by boat from other ports in the United States to be resold in New Orleans.

1856 Over the course of this year, 611 enslaved people of African descent are brought by boat from other ports in the United States to be resold in New Orleans.

1857 Emancipation of all enslaved persons is prohibited by Louisiana law and free blacks are encouraged to voluntarily enslave themselves.

Over the course of this year, 483 enslaved people of African descent are brought by boat from other ports in the United States to be resold in New Orleans.

1858 There is no record of any enslaved people of African descent being brought by boat from other ports in the United States to be resold in New Orleans for this year.

1859 In May, roughly 150 free people of color from rural parishes in southwest Louisiana depart for Haiti from the Port of New Orleans. They are fleeing racist persecution and violent attacks by bands of white vigilantes in the Opelousas area. When several of those fleeing the attacks seek refuge in New Orleans, the Haitian consul in New Orleans, P.E. Desdunes, begins recruiting free people from Louisiana to settle in Haiti with offers of free transportation to the island nation and assurances of political equality and economic opportunity. Another group of 195 free blacks from the Baton Rouge area will leave for Haiti in June, followed by smaller delegations into early 1860. Some will return to New Orleans by the fall of 1859; others will resettle in Vera Cruz, where a colony of free blacks has been established. Some of the Louisiana expatriates will establish trading relationships between New Orleans and Vera Cruz. Those who remain in Haiti also appear to prosper.

1860 The population grows to 170,024, according to the census. The Enslaved population declines for the second straight decade to 14,484 (8.5%). Free People of Color increase slightly to 10,939 (6.4%) but decline as a percentage of the population. There are 5 people listed as Other. Whites in the city now number 144,601 (85%) and the 1850s had been the decade of the greatest prosperity for whites in the history of New Orleans. Per capita wealth for white people in Louisiana is now third highest in the United States, trailing only South Carolina and Mississippi, which also have economies fueled by the labor of enslaved people. And while this is a period of increased misery for the majority of black folks, a few also prosper. By 1860, New Orleans is home to some of the wealthiest free blacks in the South. Roughly 3,000 of them own enslaved people, too. Moreover, the proportion of free people of color who are of mixed racial ancestry in Louisiana is the highest of any state in the South, at 81.3 percent, compared with 35 percent on average for free blacks in the states in the Upper South.

Over the course of this year, 417 enslaved people of African descent are brought by boat from other ports in the United States to be resold in New Orleans.

1861 Anticipating the onset of civil war, a number of the city's free blacks form the Native Guards of the Louisiana Militia at their own expense and offer their services to Confederate Louisiana. Jordan Noble (c. 1796-1890), the former drummer boy in the Battle of New Orleans in 1815, is one of the leaders of this Native Guard contingent. When Union forces occupy New Orleans the following year, the Native Guards switch over to their side. Noble was born in Georgia and moved to New Orleans in 1811. He managed to join the U.S. Army the following year and served as a drummer for the all-white Seventh Regiment during the Battle of New Orleans. He later joined General Andrew Jackson's forces when they defeated the Seminoles in Florida in 1817 and served in the Mexican War of 1846-1848. After the Civil War, "Old Jordan" will become a staunch Republican, serving as a detective in the state-run Metropolitan Police when he is well into his seventies and publishing the *Black Republican* newspaper.

1862 On May 1, Union forces under the command of General William Butler, nicknamed "Beast" by the city's white Confederate sympathizers, begin occupying New Orleans. A naval blockade of the port was established a few days prior to the land invasion. The city surrenders without a fight.

In September, Gen. Butler's forces set up temporary housing, health care and feeding programs for 10,000 enslaved people who flock to the city from rural plantations and neighboring areas when they learn that New Orleans is under Union control. In exchange for wages, food and shelter, thousands of blacks build fortifications for the army to protect the city. There isn't enough work, however, for all those who have made their way into the city. So Gen. Butler orders "idle" folks to return to their plantations.

Café du Monde Coffee Stand opens in the French Market in the Vieux Carré section of the city near the river. Though not owned by her, the coffee stand owes its existence to the pioneering efforts of a woman named Rose Nicaud, about whom few records will survive but she was likely the first person in the city to sell fresh roasted coffee from a cart, and later from a fixed stand in or near the site of the current Café du Monde, earlier in the 19th century. Nicaud is believed to have been an enslaved woman who made enough money roasting and selling coffee on Sundays to buy her freedom and later expand her business. She is one of several black women, and men, who earn their living as street vendors in the city, most notably, selling pralines and other candy, hot calas (rice cakes), coffee, fresh fruit and vegetables.

1863 Union General Nathaniel Banks, who succeeded Gen. Butler as head of the occupying force in New Orleans, orders the creation of a new fighting unit, the Corps d'Afrique, consisting of 5,000 black soldiers under the command of white officers. Altogether, 24,000 black Louisianians will fight for the Union cause during the war, the highest number from any state.

On July 29, a funeral procession through the streets of the city for Captain André Cailloux (1825-1863), the self-proclaimed "blackest man in New Orleans," draws a crowd of thousands. Cailloux, a renowned boxer and horseman, is one of the first black men to be killed in the U.S. Civil War (1861-1865). Born enslaved to a family named Duvernay that resides on the outskirts of New Orleans, the future soldier apprenticed as a cigar maker before buying his freedom in 1846 and opening his own cigar-making business. He may likely have taken the surname Cailloux (which means "stones" in French) at this time. At any rate, he learnt to read and write in both English and French, married and fathered four children, three of whom survive and are educated at the Catholic School for Indigent Orphans (Ecole des Orphelins Indigents), the educational institution that opened in 1848 with funds left by Marie Couvent, a once-enslaved free woman of color. Cailloux's wife, Felicie Coulon Cailloux, serves as principal at the school for several years, which is also a hub for the city's Afro-Creole intellectuals. Cailloux becomes a lieutenant in the Native Guard, a militia unit formed by free men of color at the outbreak of the Civil War. They pledge themselves to the Confederate cause initially but switch to the Union side when Union forces occupy New Orleans in April 1862. In September of that year, the all-black Union Army 1st Louisiana Native Guard is formed, consisting mostly of escaped slaves, and Cailloux signs on as a captain in the unit. The regiment's first major assignment is the Siege of Port Hudson, a Confederate stronghold on the Mississippi River 100 miles upriver from New

Orleans. Situated on a sharp bend south of where the Red River flows into the Mississippi, Port Hudson is fortified and protected by 6,800 Confederate troops. The Red River was a key route for sending supplies from Texas to the rebel forces. If Union forces could capture the position, they could effectively cut off the supply line. The Union sends 30,000 troops to seize the port. Eager to prove that black men will fight, even in extremely adverse situations (as if that hadn't already been proved countless times), Cailloux leads his troops early on in the campaign on several futile charges uphill against the Confederate positions, constantly urging his men to advance. He is shot and wounded but refuses to leave the field of battle. Instead, he keeps leading charges with one arm dangling from his shoulder until he is finally killed by the enemy on May 27, 1863. His corpse will lie on the battle field for nearly seven weeks before the Confederates surrender on July 9 after being starved into submission, not dislodged militarily. Cailloux's corpse is then retrieved and brought back to New Orleans for a hero's funeral.

1864 All signs advertising slaves for sale are ordered taken down throughout New Orleans, effective January 1. The bulk of the city's notorious slave pens--roughly 50 at the height of the trade--are concentrated at the edge of the Vieux Carré around Chartres and Esplanade streets and in the current Central Business District around Common Street and the waterfront. Their selling season generally runs from September through May. When the era of slave sales ends, the properties will become boarding houses and other commercial enterprises. After the rise of the domestic slave trade in the United States (when imported slaves were forbidden in the country after 1808), tens of thousands of enslaved people from places like Virginia and Maryland were sold in New Orleans at these slave pens and at marketplaces in well-known venues like the otherwise-elegant St. Louis Hotel.

Nearly 1,000 property-owning free men of color sign a petition on January 5 pleading for men of their caste to be given the right to vote--"all the citizens of Louisiana of African descent born free before the rebellion"--which they intend to deliver to the president of the United States, Abraham Lincoln. The group assigns E. Arnold Bertonneau and Jean Baptiste Roudanez to travel to Washington, DC and deliver the petition to the president. When Bertonneau and Roudanez meet with Republican Senator Charles Sumner prior to seeing The Great Emancipator, Sumner urges them to expand their demand to include suffrage for the formerly enslaved as well as free people of color. Bertonneau and Roudanez consent to the change and make their presentation to Lincoln. After their conversation, Lincoln writes to the governor of Louisiana and asks him to consider giving some black men, "the very intelligent and those who have fought gallantly in our ranks," the right to vote, which is all the free men of color from New Orleans wanted in the first place. Lincoln's suggestion is ignored, of course, but after the Civil War, all black men do gain suffrage for a few years.

On October 4, *The New Orleans Tribune (La Tribune de la Nouvelle Orléans)* becomes the first black-owned daily newspaper in the United States. Published by Louis Charles Roudanez (1823-1890), a physician whose father (Louis Roudanez) was French and mother (Aimée Potens) part-black, the *Tribune* is written in English and French. The *Tribune* advocates full suffrage and free public education, among other issues. It also serves as the official organ of the National Equal Rights League and advocates that those blacks who had been free before the Civil War have a duty to help those newly freed adjust and adapt to fruitful lives as free people (i.e., be credits to their race). Roudanez, older brother of activist Jean Baptiste Roudanez, had been a partner in a previous newspaper, *L'Union (The Union)*, which became the first black-owned newspaper to be published in Louisiana in 1862 and the first black Republican paper in the country. Created in the aftermath of the occupation of New Orleans by Union forces during the Civil War, *L'Union* advocated full equality for free men of color. It was published as a biweekly and later as a tri-weekly publication. When *L'Union* ceases publication on July, 19, 1864, due to lack of support, Roudanez launches the *Tribune*. It will eventually fold in 1870. In November 1985, another publication calling itself *The New Orleans Tribune* will be established by Kermit Thomas, James Borders, and Dwight and Beverly McKenna. It will be a monthly newsmagazine.

1865 A Louisiana branch of the Republican Party is founded five months after the end of the Civil War. The party of Abe Lincoln, the Great Emancipator, is comprised of men who were formerly enslaved as well as leading free men of color and whites from both the North and the South. Though the members of the party hold sometimes divergent views about the pace and extent of black liberation needed in the state, the whites are not as openly racist and regressive as the Democrats, who seek to keep blacks in virtual enslavement. In October, members of the First District Emancipation Club, which includes black dock workers, hold a march with black soldiers to contribute $1 per person to a fund raising effort for the Republican Central Committee. It is an early expression of black worker solidarity in the city after the War of Emancipation.

A "minor riot" occurs during a *raquette* (racket) match on September 10 on a field at the intersection of Elysian Fields and Claiborne Avenues. The event is attended by thousands of spectators and the players are both black and white. The melee results in the death of one white man and the beating of several others. The violence occurs "owing to some interference on the part of whites," the New Orleans *Picayune* reports. No arrests are made and no charges are filed relative to the incident. With rumors spreading across the city that some whites plan to retaliate the following weekend, the mayor bans the sport for several months, hoping to avoid further violence. *Raquette,* a precursor to lacrosse, was the first organized team sport in New Orleans. It had been invented by Choctaws (Chahtas) and was played on a huge field, 600 feet long by 300 feet wide, with teams of 40 players a side. In the earliest days of New Orleans, the rough and tumble contests were played at the site of what will later be called Congo Square, aka the Congo Plains. Soon free (and probably enslaved) people of color became participants as well. Over time, local white men also learn the sport. By the mid-1800s, the game's terminology has become totally creolized and the matches draw larger and larger crowds until they stop being held during the Civil War. When play picks up again in the summer of 1865, the two teams that traditionally compete against each other reorganize. One is called La Ville (The City) and the other is Bayou (The Country) and it appears that blacks and whites have no problems sharing the same field until the incident on September 10. Thereafter, the popularity of the sport declines and whites refuse for many years to play with blacks, who push forward anyway with all-colored squads. Nevertheless, by 1890, *raquette* will fade from the New Orleans sports scene as other games become more popular.

1866 Less than a year after the end of the Civil War, several free men of color incorporate the Union Sons Benevolent Association of Louisiana on March 1 and buy a parcel of property at 1309 Perdido Street on which they build a hall that serves as their organization's headquarters. When not convening their members at the hall, however, the Union Sons rent and/or use the space for other gatherings, including allowing the First Lincoln Baptist Church to hold services there on Sunday mornings and hosting dances on Saturday nights that last sometimes until the wee hours of the morning. By 1905, the Union Sons Hall will become known as the Funky Butt Hall in tribute to a blues song created by jazz progenitor Charles "Buddy" Bolden, a frequent performer at rough and rowdy dances there. In the 1920s, the space will be converted into the Greater St. Matthews Baptist Church, a full-time place of worship. In 1950, the state government will buy the property and build the Louisiana State Office Building on the site, across the street from what was then the new New Orleans City Hall.

A multiracial political gathering at the Mechanics Institute, located near the intersection of Common and Dryades Streets in the business district of the city, convenes more than 200 blacks and two dozen progressive whites--mostly members of the Republican Party--to organize efforts to increase rights for blacks in Louisiana. The fourth day of the convening, July 30, is disrupted, however, when a heavily armed gang of former Confederate soldiers (aided by local white police) confronts the attendees and indiscriminately fires upon the gathering during a parade and rally. When the smoke clears, 34 blacks and 3 white radicals have been killed in the ambush; another 100 persons have been injured. If the intent of the ambush had been to frighten the freedmen and their allies into submission, it fails (at least in the short term). Instead, the massacre garners national notoriety, helps fuel efforts to increase Republican control of Congress in 1866 and to enact the Reconstruction Bill of 1867 that provides for federal control of the South, displacement of former Confederates, and suffrage for free men of color, among other things.

Pierre Casanave, one of the city's earliest noted black undertakers, dies. With a mortuary located at the intersection of Bourbon and St. Louis Streets, Casanave, a native of Haiti, had gained attention in the 1850s and 1860s for the stylish funerals he provided and his secret but highly effective formula for embalming bodies. After Casanave dies, his sons Pierre Casanave, Jr. and Gardane Casanave operate the family funeral home into the 1880s.

1867 The U.S. Congress passes the first Reconstruction Act on March 2, which places the former Confederate states under military rule. In New Orleans, the white Democrat mayor's administration that tacitly supported the massacre of Republican activists at the Mechanics Institute in 1866 is removed from office and some Confederates are disfranchised. More importantly, the registration of black voters is authorized and a process is laid out for writing a new state constitution beginning in November 1867. The voter registration drive leads to a black electoral majority in the state and in their first exercise of this voting strength, blacks elect several delegates to the new constitutional convention.

Black citizens engage in direct action in April and May to integrate New Orleans street cars, which are pulled by mule teams. Up to this point, colored people are only permitted to ride on separate street cars designated with a star on them. They start boarding unstarred cars and refuse to get off. After some of the first integraters get booted from the street cars and arrested, other blacks begin pelting the whites-only street cars with rocks and miscellaneous objects. Fights between blacks and reactionary whites also break out around the city. Eventually, the street car company capitulates and dismantles the segregated system.

On May 15, Mayor Edward Heath, who had been placed in office by the military authorities sent in to rule the city as part of the Reconstruction Act of 1867, bars blacks from seeking service in any privately owned establishments "against the wishes and consent of the owners."

Between May 16 and 18, more than 1,000 black dock workers strike along the Mississippi River waterfront and at the New Basin Canal, demanding pay increases (from $3 per 10-hour day to $4 a day) and a more equitable system for securing work from steamboat and barge owners. U.S. Army Major General Mower sides with the workers and devises a new contracting system for the boat owners to use but he also threatens to suppress any riot with military force. Outward tensions on the waterfront subside for the time being.

The Sisters of the Holy Family, the black religious order led by now-Saint Henriette Delille, open St. Mary's School on Chartres Street, in what will become the French Quarter, to educate black girls. In 1881, the school will move into the historic Quadroon Ballroom at 717 Orleans Avenue and become St. Mary's Academy. Boarding accommodations at the new location will attract students of color from all the southern states as well as Nicaragua, British Honduras (Belize), Panama, and Spanish Honduras. By the early 1900s the enrollment will be over two hundred. In 1965, the school will move again to a new, larger campus in eastern New Orleans at 6905 Chef Menteur Boulevard. That campus will be severely flooded in the wake of Hurricane Katrina in 2005 and the school will be forced to relocate for two years. During this period, however, it will expand its services to include a co-educational pre-kindergarten-middle school component along with its all-girls high school. Enrollment will exceed 600 and the school will continue to maintain its record of high academic ratings. In September 2015, the school will venture into an entirely new undertaking when it opens a Male Academy for boys in grades 4-7.

....

1868 A revolutionary new Louisiana State Constitution is ratified by a vote of 66,000 to 49,800 in April. Black voters largely support it, white voters largely do not. Among other provisions, the new constitution guarantees equal rights and privileges to every citizen in licensed businesses, public schools and institutions of higher education, public transportation and public resorts.

Oscar James Dunn (1826-1871) is elected the first black lieutenant governor of Louisiana on June

13. Born enslaved in New Orleans, Dunn trained as a carpenter and became a leading Prince Hall Freemason. Later, he was the first former slave to be elected to the Louisiana State Senate, where he served as president pro tempore. Running on the Republican Party ticket, Dunn accepts the lieutenant governor slot when Francis Dumas, a black man who has campaigned for the party's nomination for governor, fails to win the party's endorsement and declines the offer to run as lieutenant governor. After Dunn dies in office in 1871, he will be succeeded by another black Republican, Pinckney Benton Stewart (P.B.S.) Pinchback, who will briefly serves as governor in 1872 for 34 days when the white Republican in the office, Henry Clay Warmouth, is impeached, an action Dunn works for even though he initially won office as Warmouth's running mate. Dunn's funeral is reported to have been attended by 50,000 people.

1869 Straight University is founded on June 12, making it the first of six historically black colleges that will be established in New Orleans in the 19th and 20th centuries. Straight University (1869-1934) and New Orleans University (1869-1935)--which began its existence as Union Normal School--will merge in 1935 and become Dillard University. Leland University (1870-1959) will be established in 1870 with support from Baptist missionary organizations and the Freedmen's Aid Bureau. Beginning its operation as a primary school, Leland will soon expand into a high school and later a college with a campus on St. Charles Avenue at the intersection of what will become known in later years as Newcomb Boulevard, near Audubon Park. In 1915, a major hurricane (the Great Storm of 1915) will destroy Leland's buildings and the school's directors will choose to move the campus out of New Orleans, eventually settling in Baker, LA, outside Baton Rouge. Leland will finally cease operations in 1959 due to insufficient enrollment. Southern University (1880-1914) likewise will move to the Baton Rouge area when it opens its new campus in Scotlandville on a bluff overlooking the Mississippi River in 1914. In 1925, Xavier University, the nation's first black Catholic college, will open its doors on Magazine Street in the uptown section of New Orleans at the former site of Southern University before moving to its current Gert Town neighborhood location in 1929. In 1959, Southern University at New Orleans (SUNO)--a branch of the Southern University System, which includes a campus in Shreveport as well as Scotlandville--will open on a 17-acre campus in Pontchartrain Park, the first subdivision in the city created for middle-class black families. Straight, Leland and Dillard (named for white donors) and New Orleans University are founded and funded by white Protestant church-affiliated missionary organizations. Xavier will be created by a group of Catholic nuns and Southern will be founded by the State of Louisiana. Over time, however, financial support for Straight and New Orleans University from their founding organizations will wane and the schools will be forced to consolidate their efforts in order to survive. Dillard, Xavier and SUNO continue to exist and to prepare black professionals in the 21st century.

1870 The total population stands at 191,418, according to the census: 50,456 Free Colored (26.4%), 140,923 White (73.6%) and 39 Other (.02%).

A select group of black waterfront workers forms the Screwmen's Benelovent Association No. 2. Among the diverse types of workers on the waterfront--screwmen, longshoremen, draymen, yardmen and roustabouts--screwmen are at the top of the pecking order. Working in five-man teams, their job is to tightly pack and unpack cargo, cotton mostly, using special jackscrews. White workers have already formed the Screwmen's Benelovent Association, a union and mutual aid organization. Since their jobs are the highest paying, blacks have agitated for the chance to learn the skill. The white screwmen agree to permit 100 blacks to join their trade, though not their union.

John Baptiste Jourdain (1830-1888), a Civil War veteran, is the first black detective hired by the Metropolitan Police, which is under state control during the Reconstruction era. Jourdain, the son of a white father and colored mother, joins the police force when a call for black officers is issued by the state government. Jourdain, who had become politically active after the war, will go on to win election to the Louisiana Legislature in 1874 as a Radical Republican representing the Seventh Ward of New Orleans. However, when white right-wing Democrats win control of the government in 1876, Jourdain soon loses his seat and his political clout. He is working as a part-time furniture salesman on April 4, 1888, when he commits suicide by shooting himself in the head at his family's crypt in St. Louis Cemetery #1.

The Republican-controlled state legislature orders the integration of New Orleans public schools. By the end of the year, 1,000 black children are peaceably attending classes alongside thousands of white students in nearly one-third of the city's public schools. This arrangement will last until 1876, when white Democrats win back control of the governor's office and the legislature and begin a campaign of reinstituting white supremacist policies and laws, including segregation of schools.

1872 Pinckney Benton Stewart Pinchback (1837-1921) briefly serves as governor of the State of Louisiana for 15 days, December 29, 1872, through January 13, 1873, making him the first black person to hold such a position in the United States. Born free in Macon, GA, Pinchback worked as a riverboat steward before making his way to New Orleans in 1862, where he volunteered to fight on the Union side and became company commander of the 2nd Louisiana Regiment Native Guard Infantry, made up mostly of escaped slaves. After the war, Pinchback joined the Republican Party and was elected to the Louisiana Senate in 1868. He soon became president pro tempore of the Legislature, which included 42 men of African-American descent--holding 35 of the 70 seats in the House and 7 of 36 seats in the Senate. When Lt. Governor Oscar Dunn dies in office in 1871,

Pinchback moves up to the Lt. Governor's position. He serves out the end of Governor Henry Clay Warmouth's term when the governor is impeached for corruption. Pinchback will go on to have a career as a newspaper publisher (the biweekly *New Orleans Louisianian*), a surveyor of customs in New Orleans, and a U.S. Marshal in New York.

In April, approximately 200 black waterfront workers form the Longshoremen's Protective Union; the following year, white workers form the Longshoremen's Benevolent Association. The longshoremen's union is one of 15 black labor unions in New Orleans operating between 1865 and 1880.

1873 Caesar Carpentier Antoine (1836–1921) begins a four-year term as lieutenant governor of Louisiana. He is the third (and last?) Afro-Louisianian elected to the office, after Oscar Dunn and P.B.S. Pinchback. A veteran of the Civil War and a business leader, C.C. Antoine was born in New Orleans but will later relocate to Shreveport in North Louisiana, where he will die and be buried. He co-founded *The Black Republican* weekly newspaper with Jordan Noble in 1865 and will be a noted horseman, planter, grocer and investor in ventures such as railroads.

George Geddes Sr. (1845-1916) establishes a mortuary business with headquarters on Rampart Street that will spawn an empire of family-led businesses operating successfully for more than a century. After the elder Geddes dies, his son Joseph (1880-1948) will take over the George D. Geddes Company and rename it the Joseph P. Geddes Funeral Home. Another son, George Jr. (1871-1902), will establish a funeral home named for himself; it will become Geddes-Richards Funeral Home after his death and last until the 1970s. In the most enduring venture, Clement J. Geddes (1877-1913) will form a partnership with civic leader and businessman Arnold Moss in 1909, Geddes & Moss Undertaking Parlor. When Clement dies, his share of the business will go to his widow Gertrude Pocté Geddes (1878-1970). She and Moss will later launch their own insurance company, which proves to be successful. George Geddes Sr. will be the founding president of the Unity Life Insurance Company in 1907, which becomes the largest of the city's black-owned insurers. In 1919, the widowed Gertrude Geddes will marry William Willis, a dentist and businessman who dies in 1947. After partner Arnold Moss (1869-1931) dies, she will change the name of the business to Gertrude Geddes Willis Funeral Home and Life Insurance Company. Joseph Misshore Jr. (1932-2008), Willis' grand-nephew, will succeed her as head of the company; his son Joseph III will succeed him. Though the Gertrude Geddes Willis Life Insurance Company will become insolvent in 2013 and its outstanding policies get transferred to black-owned Majestic Life Insurance Company in 2015, Gertrude Geddes Willis will still remembered as likely the first black woman in New Orleans to become a millionaire through her business dealings. At the time of her death, her various enterprises will employ more than 150 people and operate the largest black-owned funeral parlor in New Orleans.

"An Appeal for the Unification of the People of Louisiana" is promulgated by a bi-racial coalition spearheaded by bi-racial landowner/philanthropist Alexandre Aristide Mary (1823-1891) and former Confederate General P.G.T. Beauregard, who commanded the opening attack of the Civil War at Fort Sumpter, SC. The manifesto is signed by over 1,800 black and white citizens and calls for a statewide commitment to civil rights for all. It presages the Civil Rights Acts of 1875 and 1964, according to some historians, but gains no traction around the state. As a result, the Unification Movement collapses and white supremacist-instigated racial strife continues.

....

1874 On September 14, 5,000-8,000 former Confederate soldiers and reactionary white Democrats launch an attempted coup d'etat against the sitting governor of Louisiana, William Pitt Kellogg and his black lieutenant governor, C.C. Antoine. The insurgents attack the troops guarding the Custom House on Canal Street, where Kellogg is stationed. The forces there are comprised of the mostly black state-controlled Metropolitan Police force of 500, 3,000 black militiamen and 100 other police. The white military force overruns the black forces, seizes the Customs House and an ammunitions storehouse, ousts Gov. Kellogg and proclaims their own man, John McEnery, governor. The event has been remembered as the Battle of Liberty Place. Eleven blacks and 16 whites are killed in the fighting. The white supremacist victory lasts three days. Federal troops are sent in to beat back the insurgents, many of whom are members of a local Ku Klux Klan-like organization called the White League that has been drilling and preparing their offensive for months. Though Louisiana is roughly half black at this time, whites are three times as numerous as blacks in New Orleans. While the state government is controlled by Republicans, Democrats--the party of white ex-Confederates and their sympathizers--control elective offices in New Orleans, including the mayor's office. Though this military battle to reinstate white racist control of Louisiana fails to sustain its objectives, the white supremacist campaign continues through other means.

Felicie Coulon Cailloux, widow of Civil War hero Captain André Cailloux, dies in poverty working as a domestic servant for the priest who delivered the eulogy at her husband's funeral. The first teacher and the first principal of the Catholic School for Indigent Orphans, she had struggled for several years to secure a pension from the U.S. government based on her husband's service. When the pension does come through, it is apparently not sufficient to support her and her three children.

The Freedmen's Savings and Trust Company, chartered by Congress in March 1865 to help black veterans and other freed people build savings, fails during a national depression that grips the U.S. from

1873 to 1877. The Freedmen's Savings clientele across Louisiana, including New Orleans, lose $300,000 ($6.8 million in 2015 dollars) in savings.

....

1875 Thirteen black baseball clubs in New Orleans form a citywide league.

....

1876 Francois Lacroix (c. 1810-1876), one of the wealthiest black New Orleanians of his era, dies. A dry-goods merchant, tailor, real estate investor, slave owner and philanthropist, Lacroix was born to free parents from Haiti who had been exiled to Cuba before finding refuge in New Orleans. In 1860, Lacroix's estate was valued at $262,000 (approximately $7.5 million in 2015 dollars). Among his more notable real estate holdings are a horse racing course on Gentilly Boulevard that will become the site of the Fair Grounds, the third oldest race track in the nation. A widower at the time of his passing, Lacroix's son Victor was one of the scores of progressive black people murdered by reactionary white supremacists during the Mechanics Institute massacre on July 30, 1866.

....

1877 Federal troops are withdrawn from New Orleans and the rest of the South in April as Reconstruction comes to an end and white supremacy is structurally reinstated in Louisiana. On March 2, Republican Rutherford B. Hayes was declared winner of the 1876 presidential election over Democrat Samuel J. Tilden, even though Tilden had won the popular vote 50.1 to 47.95%. However, a special U.S. congressional panel had awarded Florida's electors to Hayes, giving him the victory in the Electoral College vote. The Democrats agree to accept the decision if Hayes will withdraw federal troops from the South and, in effect, return it to white supremacist control.

Cornetist Charles "Buddy" Bolden is born on September 6. He will become an exceptionally forceful, loud-playing musician and leader of a band that is credited with being the first to play the music that came to be known as jazz. "King" Bolden, the first man to perform improvised solos in and around ensemble arrangements, never made any recordings, however, and will die on November 4, 1931, at the Insane Asylum of Louisiana in Jackson, LA, where he will be committed in 1907 due to what family members and friends consider erratic and dangerous behavior. Bolden, whose last public performance will end when he drops out part of the way through the city's 1906 Labor Day Parade, is the prototype for the dissolute jazz musician stereotype that will become commonplace in the 20th century--immensely talented and path-breaking but driven, hard-living, substance-abusing and cursed with a meteoric, path-breaking rise to prominence coupled with a catastrophic fall too early in life. Bolden will be remembered in tales of his musical exploits and in at least one song about him. According to this lore, one night the cornetist and his band were playing at the Union Sons Hall when a foul stench seemed to linger in the air. The odor failed to dissipate and the Bolden band began improvising a song that has been memorialized as "Buddy Bolden's Blues" or "Funky

Butt." The original lyrics of the song had been a tribute to President Abraham Lincoln's role in freeing the enslaved. "I thought I heer'd Abe Lincoln shout/ Rebels, close down them plantations and let all them niggers out./ I'm positively sure I heer'd Mr. Lincoln shout." On the night in question, however, someone in the Bolden band substituted these words instead: "I thought I heard Buddy Bolden shout/ Open up that window and let that bad air out./ Open up that window and let that foul air out." Another verse was "I thought I heard Buddy Bolden say/Funky butt, funky butt/Take it away." The song went on in this manner and other coarse, raunchy, ribald lyrics got added over time--to the delight of the listening public for generations to come.

....

1879 The Excelsior Brass Band is founded by Théogène Baquet and later becomes acknowledged as one of the pioneers of the New Orleans jazz sound. Baquet will lead the band, which generally featured 10-12 musicians, until 1904. George Moret will take over until 1922 and Peter Bocage will be in charge until the Excelsior dissolves in 1931.

....

1880 The U.S. Census Bureau reports that the population of New Orleans is 216,090: 57,617 Negro--used for the first time (26.7%), 158,367 (73.3%) White and 106 Other (.05%).

....

1881 Black dock workers join forces with white dock workers to successfully strike for higher wages and other employment protections on the New Orleans waterfront in September. Ten months earlier, in December 1880, the workers banded into an interracial corps of 13,000 members and created the Cotton Men's Executive Council, an umbrella organization of more than 30 smaller unions covering the whole gamut of tasks performed on the waterfront. When negotiations with steamboat owners and cotton press owners fail to produce results, the workers go on strike. The agreements that come out of the massive work stoppage also result in a common wage standard for each class of waterfront laborer and bar employers from paying non-union workers lower wages. These were gains individual black unions had been unsuccessful in achieving on their own despite launching a series of strikes since 1865.

The Central Trades and Labor Assembly is formed on November 25, 1881. This interracial federation includes waterfront, railroad and warehouse workers as well as people working in other fields such as construction, printing and journalism. The large assembly will later display its worker unity in annual parades each November from 1881 through 1888. Though blacks will never be elected president of the assembly, they will serve as vice presidents and other officers. One labor leader will later declare that the assembly had "done more to break the color line in New Orleans than any other thing" since the emancipation of the enslaved.

1882 The Cosmopolitan Insurance Association is founded with $25,000 ($610,000 in 2015 dollars) in capital stock. C.C. Antoine is president of the venture. J.B. Gaudet is vice president, William G. Brown is treasurer and Aristide Dejoie is secretary. In later years, Dejoie will continue innovating ways to grow black-owned insurance companies.

....

1884 Duplain Rhodes Sr. (1866-1938) launches The Rhodes Undertaking Company. The company will continue to be family-owned into the 21st century with Duplain Rhodes Jr. (1899-1988) providing long-time leadership and overseeing expansions into life insurance and limousine services before handing the reins of the enterprises over to his children. Rhodes and Charbonnet-Labat, founded in 1887 as Labat & Ray, will emerge as the city's pre-eminent black undertakers in the post-Katrina era.

The first world's fair to be held in New Orleans, the World Cotton Centennial, opens on December 16 at Upper City Park, the site of present-day Audubon Park, and runs through June 2, 1885. At the time, nearly one-third of all cotton produced in the United States is handled in the port and warehouses of New Orleans. The city also is home to the Cotton Exchange, which facilitates and helps regulate the trade of cotton. Black businessman and civic leader James Lewis (c. 1832-1914) operates the Experimental Restaurant on the fair grounds to ensure his people receive decent food service in hospitable accommodations. Northern visitors and Europeans repeatedly remark on the number of well-dressed, well-behaved black patrons strolling the fair grounds and the apparent lack of antagonism toward them by southern whites.

....

1885 The Young Men Olympian Jr. Benevolent Association is formally incorporated on August 23 to provide financial safety nets to its members by creating pools of funds to pay for burials and major medical expenses. At the time the organization is founded, some insurance companies refuse to sell health or burial policies to blacks, so community members create their own solutions. The Young Men Olympian is the oldest surviving social aid & pleasure club in New Orleans. The organization also sponsors an annual parade--a second line--to celebrate its founding. By 2015, there will be more than 40 clubs that sponsor annual second lines on Sunday afternoons throughout the year. The parades will become colorful affairs filled with the sounds of brass bands, energetic dancing in the street, and colorful, coordinated ensembles worn by organization members.

....

1886 According to an article printed on December 4 in the white-owned *Daily Picayune*, "(I)n New Orleans a very large proportion of skilled labor in the house-building trades, such as carpentry, bricklaying, plastering, and painting, is performed by colored mechanics. Many of the most important public and private buildings in this city have been chiefly, if not wholly erected by the labor of colored men."

....

1889 *The Daily Crusader* newspaper is founded by Louis Martinet, attorney and activist. *The Crusader*'s motto is "A Free Vote and Fair Count, Free Schools, Fair Wages, Justice and Equal Rights." The paper's office later serves as a meeting place for members of the Citizens Committee (Comité des Citoyens), which orchestrates legal challenges to racial segregation. *The Crusader* ceases publication in 1896 after the U.S. Supreme Court decrees racial segregation to be lawful in the *Plessy v Ferguson* case that originated in New Orleans.

The Flint Medical College of New Orleans University is established. It will produce 116 graduates before closing in 1911 due to financial shortfalls. The medical school has been funded by the Freemen's Aid Society, a program of the Methodist Episcopal Church. Ella Prescott (1876-1925), class of 1904, will be the first woman to practice medicine in Louisiana.

1890 The total population of New Orleans is 242,039, according to the census: 64,491 Negro (26.6%), 177,376 White (73.3%) and 172 Other (.1%).

Louisiana Legislative Code 111, the Separate Car Act, is enacted. It requires "equal, but separate" train car accommodations for whites and coloreds. Violations of the law are considered misdemeanors and are punishable by a $25 fine or up to 20 days in jail. More crucially, the act also declares that a person with any African ancestry is a Negro. This "one drop" rule officially abolishes all legal distinctions between pure blacks and mixed race people, i.e., mulattos/ quadroons/octoroons, etc. Anyone with a drop of black blood will be considered black. The law reinforces the defeat of previous efforts in 1864 to declare that any person with one-fourth or less of black blood be considered white.

1891 The Citizens Committee (Comité des Citoyens) is formed in New Orleans to combat Louisiana's growing assault on the political rights and socio-economic opportunities of its black citizens, particularly Louisiana Legislative Code 111, popularly known as the Separate Car Act. Alexander Aristide Mary, a former gubernatorial candidate, along with 17 other black leaders constitute the group's founders. The avowed mission of the Citizens Committee is "to protest the adoption and enforcement of the statutes that established the unjust and humiliating discrimination against the Black race in Louisiana." The committee immediately challenges the segregation laws when Daniel Desdunes, son of one of the founding members, author Rodolphe Desdunes, is arrested when he takes a seat in a whites-only car of an interstate train as part of a plan to challenge the constitutionality of the law. Desdunes and the Citizens Committee win their case. The results will be different, however, when they challenge segregation on intrastate travel in Louisiana in the infamous *Plessy v Ferguson* case in 1896. Mary, however, will not live to see the outcome of the case. He will commit suicide in New York in 1891.

1892 Canadian George "Little Chocolate" Dixon (1870-1908), the first black man to be a world boxing champion, successfully defends his world featherweight title against Jack Skelly, a white American boxer, by administering a brutal beating to his opponent before knocking him out in the eighth round at the Olympic Club, 2725 Royal Street on September 6. This is the first time black spectators are admitted to the Olympic and the last time a black fighter is matched against a white in New Orleans until well into the next century.

Between November 8 and 12, black workers take part in a general strike involving more than 25,000 New Orleans workers from 46 unions in various industries. The strike results in wage increases for some workers and the reduction of the work day to 10 hours, but it fails to win the workers' goal to have employment limited only to union members. That concession will permit employers to drive a wedge between workers by using non-unionized black workers whenever smaller strikes occur, which erodes the interracial solidarity of the laboring classes and the clout of the labor unions.

1893 Businessman Thomy Lafon (1810-1893) dies on December 22 and leaves the bulk of his $500,000 estate to charity (equivalent to $13.1 million in 2015 dollars). It is the largest donation ever made by a black American philanthropist up to that time. Born poor to a free mother of Haitian descent and a father who was French, Lafon started his career selling cakes to working men. He then opened a shop in the city's French Quarter. In 1868, he started dealing in real estate. Lafon never married, lived modestly and consistently supported organizations working for the liberation of black people.

....

1894 The Cotton Men's Executive Council dissolves on October 17 due to interracial strife and a scramble for employment among its union members in the midst of a major U.S. depression that ravages the economy from 1893 to 1897. Black workers are beaten, chased and shot in October and November of 1894 and again in March of 1895. The attacks will be characterized as race riots and will mark the end of interracial labor cooperation for several years.

....

1895 *The Monthly Review* publishes *Violets and Other Tales*, a collection of poems and stories by New Orleanian Alice Ruth Moore, later Dunbar-Nelson (1875-1935). The young author has been teaching in the city's public school system after graduating from Straight University in 1892. Soon after the publication of this first book, Moore will leave New Orleans for Boston and then Brooklyn. In 1898, she will marry Paul Laurence Dunbar, then America's premier black poet. They will separate in 1902 and Dunbar will die in 1906. In 1916, Alice Dunbar will marry poet and civil rights activist Robert Nelson. They will stay together for the rest of her career as writer, editor and activist. In 1917, her "People of Color in Louisiana" article will be published in *The Journal of Negro History*.

The Illinois Club begins producing debutante balls each carnival season. The club is founded by Wiley Knight (1877-1953), a Tennessee native who moved to

New Orleans in 1894 after living in Chicago. Shortly after his arrival in the Crescent City, Knight opens a dance and etiquette school for people of color. The group's name reportedly derives from the fact that many of its founding members work as porters on the Illinois Central Railroad line that runs between New Orleans and Chicago. The organization will splinter in 1925 (reportedly over the choice for queen) with the breakaway group calling itself the Young Men Illinois Club. The other faction then begins calling itself the Original Illinois Club. Both factions continue to present annual balls at which respectable young ladies are introduced to society with pageantry and pomp. In just a few years, they will be joined by several other black organizations that also begin producing annual debutante or carnival balls. For his pioneering efforts, Wiley Knight is remembered as the "Father of Negro Society in New Orleans."

St. Katherine's Catholic Church opens as the first parish in the city dedicated exclusively to black and multiracial parishioners. It is located on Tulane Avenue at the corner of Marais Street. The structure was originally built in 1846 and named St. Joseph Catholic Church. When the St. Joseph parish outgrew that facility and built themselves a larger church a few blocks down Tulane Avenue, the old building was handed down to the Negroes. St. Katherine's will be demolished in 1966 after suffering damage from Hurricane Betsy in 1965.

1896 On May 18, the United States Supreme Court rules in *Plessy v Ferguson* that racial segregation is legal in public facilities as long as there are "separate but equal accommodations." The ruling was prompted by a New Orleans shoemaker, Homère (Homer) Plessy (1862-1925), a very light-skinned (7/8 white) black man who is a member of the Citizens Committee, which arranges to have him arrested in 1892 for refusing to leave his seat in a whites-only railroad car in defiance of the 1890 Louisiana Separate Car Act that segregates railroad passengers by race. John Ferguson, a judge for the Orleans Parish Criminal Court, convicts Plessy of violating the law. The case is appealed to the U.S. Supreme Court, which upholds Ferguson's ruling and creates the legal justification for racial segregation to be enacted throughout the United States, and especially in the American South, for the next 70 years.

Vitascope Hall, the nation's first movie theater, opens on Canal Street to show silent motion pictures. It quickly becomes segregated but over the next 50+ years more than 50 single-screen movie theaters are built to serve nearly every neighborhood in the city. Former vaudeville theaters like the Lyric and the Iroquois that exclusively offer live entertainment also begin showing movies and they slowly squeeze out the live acts, especially after movies with sound are introduced in 1929. As racial segregation laws and practices harden in the city, the theaters try various approaches to keep audiences separated. At some, like the Orpheum, located just off Canal Street, blacks are permitted to sit only in the balcony. At other theaters like the Isis on Dryades Street, which has no balcony, a roped-off section is provided for black patrons. Over time, such theaters as the Gallo, Lincoln, Caffin, Clabon, Circle and Carver grow to serve a black clientele almost exclusively and become significant social gathering centers in the community. By the late 1970s, however, these neighborhood theaters will be all but extinct.

1897 The Thomy Lafon School, named for the New Orleans black philanthropist who funded the construction, opens at the intersection of Howard (current-day LaSalle) and Harmony Streets. It is one of the best educational facilities of its day and reaches an enrollment of more than 900 students before it is burned down in 1900 by vindictive whites.

1898 (White) Storyville officially opens for business on New Year's Day. Situated just outside the old French Quarter and fronting on Basin Street, "The District" is an 18-block area of the city in which prostitution is permitted by ordinance of the New Orleans City Council. Another, smaller area dubbed Black Storyville also begins to operate unofficially a few blocks away on the uptown side of Canal Street. Accommodating more than 2,200 registered sex workers in its heyday, (White) Storyville's offerings are restricted to white customers, though there are black prostitutes of all shades and black madams who operate brothels servicing these white clients. It is against the law for black and white prostitutes to occupy the same premises and for blacks and whites to have sexual intercourse, but no one bothers to enforce the latter restriction in "The District." Among the more well-known and successful black madams in (White) Storyville are Willie Piazza (?-1932), who claims to be octoroon and not Sicilian despite her last name, and Lulu White (1864 or 1868-1931), who operates the opulent four-story Mahogany Hall and boasts of having the world's most alluring octoroons in her employ--40 of them working out of 15 bedrooms and 5 parlors. Emma Johnson is less widely known but her "House of all Nations" brothel specializes in exhibitions of fetishism, sadomasochism, voyeurism, virgin-selling, the sexual exploitation of children and more. (She is also infamous for offering "one on the house" to any man who can have sex with her for more than one minute with having an orgasm.) In Black Storyville, the clientele and the prostitutes are black-only and the brothels are not nearly as fancy or well-furnished as those in its more notorious white counterpart. The city will finally officially acknowledge the black district in 1917 when it decrees that all black prostitutes have to relocate there by March 1, 1917. However, after the U.S. Navy opens a base in New Orleans preparing sailors to fight in World War I, it orders New Orleans' "supermarket of sin" shut down in November 1917 in an effort to protect the health and morals of American warriors. Today, the Storyville districts, named for Alderman Sidney Story, who led the effort to have vice in the city confined to specific locales, are also remembered for promulgating a sensationalized version of voodoo--"the official religion of Storyville"--and for the role their saloons and whorehouses played in providing employment opportunities to local musicians who continued developing a distinctive sound that came to be known almost universally as jass or jazz.

The Constitution of the State of Louisiana includes a provision (Article 197), effective September 1, 1898, known as "The Grandfather Clause." It is intended to deprive black citizens of the right to vote. Grandfather Clauses were passed in Louisiana and six other Southern states. Under the new provision, voters are required to demonstrate literacy in their native tongue or to own $300 worth of property and to pay a poll tax after 1900. However, those who had enjoyed the right to vote prior to 1867, or their direct descendants, would be exempt from educational, property, or tax requirements for voting. Because former slaves were not granted the vote until the adoption of the Fifteenth Amendment in 1870, the Grandfather Clause effectively excludes most blacks from voting while providing that opportunity to many impoverished and illiterate whites. In Louisiana, the damage wreaked by this change in the state constitution is tremendous. In 1896, there are 130,334 registered black voters. Two years later, there will be only 5,320 registered black voters. By 1910, 730. In 1915, the U.S. Supreme Court will declare the Grandfather Clause unconstitutional because it violates equal voting rights guaranteed by the Fifteenth Amendment. The battle to secure the vote again, however, will be long, arduous and deadly.

1900 The total population of New Orleans is 287,104, according to the census: 77,714 Negro (27%), 208,946 White (72.9%) and 444 Other (.1%).

Robert Charles (c. 1865-1900) is a 34-year-old laborer from Mississippi who moved to New Orleans in 1894 and joined the International Migration Society in 1896 with the intent of moving to Africa in the wake of the *Plessy v Ferguson* decision. Those plans change on July 23, 1900, however, when he shoots a white policeman during a confrontation in which three police officers investigate a report of "two suspicious looking negroes" sitting on a stoop at 2800 Dryades Street in an uptown white neighborhood. Charles and his roommate Larry Pierce tell the officers they are waiting for a friend, a maid who works nearby, to get off work. Nevertheless, a scuffle ensues between Charles and one of the officers. Both men are armed and end up shooting each other in the leg. Charles flees to his residence, where he is later confronted by more officers. He shoots four more policemen, killing two, before fleeing the site. A manhunt ensues and a $250 reward is offered his capture. Five days later, on July 27, Charles is found at 1208 South Saratoga Street, where he again shoots it out with the police and the crowd of whites that had gathered. By now he has a Winchester rifle and a forge to make his own bullets. Frustrated by Charles's ability to ward off their charges, the police set fire to the building where he is holed up. He is shot when attempting to escape the smoke and flames. The mob seizes his body and continues shooting and pummeling his corpse. Before being killed, Charles, whom the New Orleans *Picayune* calls "the boldest, most desperate and dangerous Negro ever known in Louisiana," shot a total of 27 white people in the course of the week, seven lethally, including four policemen. Mobs of whites begin retaliating against any blacks they came across beginning on July 25, when three blacks are killed and more than 50 people injured. After Charles' death, there is more rioting by whites; black property is burned, including the three-year-old Thomy Lafon School, and several more blacks are beaten and wounded until a special force of 1,500 police and militia restore order. On September 2, Fred Clark, a black man who informed the police of Charles' hiding place, is shot dead by a neighbor. That neighbor, Lewis Forstall, who had deplored Clark's treachery, will be convicted of manslaughter in 1902 and sentenced to seven years in prison.

In the wake of the Robert Charles incident, public education for blacks is no longer provided beyond the fifth grade until 1917, when a former white elementary school will become McDonogh #35, the first black public high school in the city and state.

1902 The Dock and Cotton Council, an alliance of all 36 labor unions serving workers at the Port of New Orleans, agrees to share work assignments on a 50-50 basis between black and white workers. The agreement, which resurrects the interracial cooperation of the 1880s on the New Orleans waterfront, stays in place until 1923, when the New Orleans Steamship

Association wins a major strike and secures the power to disregard the waterfront unions in hiring workers and setting the terms of employment. Without union protections, however, black workers will be used as the cheapest labor force in the marketplace and will complain of being forced into "semi-slavery."

Lincoln Park, an amusement center for black patrons featuring a skating rink, dance hall, outdoor music hall, merry-go-round and hot-air balloon rides, opens in July and will continue functioning until 1930. Located on a square block bordered by Carrollton Avenue, Short (present-day Oleander), and Forshey Streets, the park will have a 15-cent admission price and will be the site of many dances, picnics, concerts and other events sponsored by social organizations. Though the park's clientele is black, the property is owned by the Standard Brewing Company, a white business. The amusement center's "unofficial manager" and one of its balloon pilots, however, is a black man called Buddy Bartley, the "colored aeronaut." Located directly across the street from Lincoln Park on the square bounded by Short, Fern, Oleander and Forshey Streets is Johnson Park, which opens in April 1902 primarily as a baseball field. Named for former Storyville waiter and saloon owner George W. Johnson, who leased the big lot across the street from his drinking establishment, Johnson Park will only exist until 1909 at the latest but it will earn a permanent place in the history of jazz. Jazz pioneer Charles "Buddy" Bolden is reputed to have initiated band battles by setting up in Johnson Park and blowing his hot, bluesy trumpet in the direction of Lincoln Park when its featured musical attraction was the popular and smooth-playing John Robichaux Orchestra or some other refined-sounding band. Bolden's intent was to draw the crowd over to his side of the street. He is reported to have described it as "calling my children home." He wins so many of these battles, he earns the nickname "King Bolden" and becomes the first giant of New Orleans jazz.

1903 An estimated 10,000-12,000 black members from 20 unions march in the Central Labor Union's Labor Day Parade on September 7. The all-black Central Labor Union (CLU) was chartered by the American Federation of Labor (AFL) in June 1901. Black labor leaders had demanded the CLU be established as a response to the AFL permitting the Central Trades and Labor Council (CTLC) to be created in 1899 as a whites-only body. In 1903, 20,000 white CTLC members from 37 unions march in their own Labor Day parade. The separate parades will become an annual tradition.

1904 Dixie Park, "For Colored People Only," opens in the Mid-City section of New Orleans on Bienville Street between Murat and Olympia. It features nightly dancing, vaudeville acts and screenings of "moving pictures" all for the admission price of 15 cents, just like its chief competitor, Lincoln Park in the Uptown section of the city. Dixie Park will stay open until 1914.

1905 The Dryades Street YMCA opens for use by black people. As the Colored Y, the organization quickly assumes a pivotal role in the community, operating such programs as a School of Commerce, a Neighborhood Youth Corps Out-of-School project, Competitive Physical Education, and youth clubs and activities. The facility also serves as a key meeting space for civic and political organizations as well as social groups. In 2000, a fire will burn down the original facility but by 2013 it will have been rebuilt four times larger as a $15 million, 80,000-square-foot facility with a six-lane indoor pool, gymnasium, fitness center and enough classroom space to house an elementary charter school.

1906 A new Thomy Lafon school is built at S. Robertson Street between Seventh and Eighth streets, replacing the first Lafon School that was burned down by rioting racists in 1900. In a pattern that will repeat itself several times throughout the rest of the 20th century, unfortunately, the second Lafon School is constructed on a toxic site--in this case a former cemetery that had been shuttered in 1879 due to unsanitary conditions. A third, modernist Lafon Elementary School will be built on the site in 1954. It will be demolished in 2011.

1907 A segregated Thomy Lafon Playground opens at the intersection of Magnolia and Sixth streets, adjacent to the Lafon School. The New Orleans Playground Commission is authorized to operate it. In 1915, noted educator Sylvanie Williams and attorney James Madison Vance organize the Colored Playground

Board and raise $500 from the black community for new playground equipment. The City of New Orleans pays for sidewalks and new curbs. The resulting facility is praised as one of the best playgrounds in the nation.

Aristide Dejoie (1847-1917), founder and president of the New Orleans chapter of the National Business League, along with several other business leaders founds Unity Industrial Life Insurance Company through a merger of several local benevolent societies' burial funds. Though the black-owned Cosmopolitan Insurance Association was formed in 1882, Unity is the first of several black insurance companies that will emerge in the city in the early decades of the 20th century, when the industry grows into a significant economic force in the black community. Among others who make notable contributions in this industry, Walter L. Cohen Sr. (1860-1930) will head a group that founds People's Life Insurance Company (later People's Industrial Life) in 1910 and surgeon Rivers Frederick (1874-1954) will head a group that launches Louisiana Industrial Life in 1920. Smith W. Green (1861-1946), the richest Afro-Orleanian of his era with an estimated $10 million in assets ($123.6 million in 2015 dollars), and his associates form Liberty Industrial Life Insurance the same year. In 1924, physician Clarence C. Haydel (1896-1982) establishes Standard Industrial Life Insurance. Aristide Dejoie's sons, Paul H. (1872-1921) and Constant C. Sr. (1881-1970), will serve as Unity Industrial Life's first two presidents. Despite experiencing rapid growth in the 1920s, Unity's fortunes will flag during the Great Depression of the 1930s and a majority stake in the company will end up being sold to a larger white firm, First National Life Insurance. Other companies will fare better and the number of local black insurers will triple by the early 1950s.

1908 Samuel Kindle, 23, is charged with assaulting Andrew Lambias, a 25-year-old white male, during a confrontation on Mardi Gras with a group of black people masking as Indians. The incident takes place at the intersection of Burgundy and Mandeville streets in the middle of the afternoon. Lambias suffers cuts and bruises about the face and head and is taken to Charity Hospital for treatment. In addition to Kindle, six other black maskers are arrested and charged with fighting and disturbing the peace. The rest of the members in their party escape capture by the police.

1909 A Mardi Gras marching troupe calling itself the Zulus appears for the first time on February 23. Led by John L. Metoyer and William Story, that year's king, the group formed the previous year under the name of the Tramps but changes its name after seeing a musical comedy at the Pythian Temple that features a character called King Zulu. In 1916, the organization will incorporate as the Zulu Social Aid and Pleasure Club. They make their mark masking in grass skirts and wearing blackface. Their high pointwill be when entertainer Louis Armstrong serves as king in 1949. After falling into decline in the 1960s, when Zulu will fail to honor a Carnival Blackout (a civil rights boycott of Mardi Gras) in 1961 and many black leaders declare it embarrassing and counterproductive to have black people parading around in blackface, Zulu will begin growing again in the 1970s and will emerge as a major Carnival organization again by the end of the 20th century.

On August 18, the New Orleans branch of the Colored Order of the Knights of Pythia, a national fraternal order, benevolent society and social organization, formally dedicates the Pythian Temple at 234 Loyola Avenue. Costing $201,000 to construct ($5.5 million in 2015 dollars), the six-story building is the largest, most expensive structure ever developed by an African-American organization in the United States. In addition to its own organizational offices, the building provides office space for insurance companies, a newspaper, a barber shop, an opera house/theater and a roof garden that is renowned for dances featuring the Pythian Orchestra, led by Manuel Perez. Though the New Orleans Knights of Pythia will report having more than 8,900 members in 1925, the Pythian Temple will close temporarily at the end of 1926 due to financial difficulties and then reopen as Piron's Garden of Joy with bandleader A.J. Piron as a part owner and bandleader. By the 1930s, Piron's Garden of Joy will close, and the Knights of Pythia lose the building by 1941. In the mid-1940s, Higgins Industries, the New Orleans firm that manufactures the ramp-bowed landing boats used to bring troops ashore during World War II, will set up a hiring office in the building. After the war, the temple building will continue housing many other businesses, including the Bank of Louisiana, before being shuttered near the end of the 20ᵗʰ century.

The Knights of Peter Claver, the largest and oldest national society for black Catholic lay people committed to doing good deeds in their communities, is founded in Mobile, AL but will later establish its national headquarters in New Orleans. In 1951, the organization will purchase the former French Society hospital building, a three-story structure built in 1861 in the 1800 block of Orleans Avenue. It will provide office space for the Knights of Peter Claver as well as other civic and political organizations, including the NAACP and the Urban League. In 1976, the Knights will build a new national headquarters next door to the older building, which will be demolished in 1983 after several attempts to preserve it.

St. Dominic's Catholic Church opens in the Carrollton section of the city to serve black parishioners, the second exclusively black parish in the city. It is later renamed St. Joan of Arc.

1910 The total population of New Orleans is 339,075, according to the census: 89,262 Negro (26.3%), 249,403 White (73.6%) and 410 Other (.1%).

1911 Rodolphe Desdunes (1849-1928) publishes *Nos Hommes et Notre Histoire* (Our People and Our History) in Montreal. The book is a nostalgic chronicle of Afro-Creole culture as exemplified in the achievements of 50 19ᵗʰ century individuals and their families, including the two Basiles--composer Basile Barrés and fencing master Basile Crokère. Desdunes' primary occupation was clerk for the U.S. Customs Service, but his civic duties included being one of the organizers of the Citizens Committee, which orchestrated Homère Plessy's 1892 challenge to racial segregation on intrastate train travel, resulting in the devastating 1896 ruling by the U.S. Supreme Court in the *Plessy v Ferguson* case that "separate but equal" accommodations for the races was legal. Desdunes will also be an editorial contributor to *The Crusader,* published by noted activist/lawyer Louis Martinet.

1913 Educator, penal reformer, and philanthropist Frances Joseph-Gaudet (1861-1934) publishes her autobiography *He Leadeth Me.* A native of Holmesville, Mississippi, Joseph-Gaudet moved to New Orleans to attend Straight University. By the time her autobiography is published, she is a divorced mother of three who has raised $5,000 and purchased a farm on Gentilly Road which she transforms into the Colored Normal and Industrial School in 1902. The facility serves as an orphanage and boarding school for children with working mothers. It eventually encompasses 105 acres and numerous buildings. In 1919, Joseph-Gaudet, then serving as the school's founding principal, will donate the facility to the Episcopal Diocese of Louisiana, which renames it to honor her. The Gaudet School will close in the 1950s, but will reorganize in 1954 as the Gaudet Episcopal Home, serving African American children 4–16 years of age. When the home closes in 1966, the land will be sold and the proceeds used to fund scholarships for needy youth.

1914 The Autocrat Club opens in a building on Claiborne Avenue and St. Phillip Street. Starting out as just a place for a few guys to play cards, it soon becomes a social hub for blacks in the downtown section of the city. In 1925, club members build a new home for the organization at 1725 St. Bernard Avenue and it begins hosting a wider range of events and social gatherings.

Harry "The Black Panther" Wills (1889-1958), a 6' 2", 209-pound New Orleans native, wins the World Colored Heavyweight Boxing Championship in his hometown on May 1. He will lose the title in his next bout in November but will regain the crown briefly in 1916 before losing it again in his second defense. Though Jack Johnson is the acknowledged world heavyweight champion during this period, he refuses to fight any black challengers during his reign, despite having once held the World Colored Heavyweight belt. The World Colored boxing titles were established when interracial fights were banned in many states, including Louisiana. New Orleans will be a frequent site for World Colored title fights in several weight classes and at several local venues into the 1940s. Eddie Palmer (1892-?), another New Orleans native, will win both the World Colored Welterweight and Middleweight titles during his career. Palmer will relocate to Philadelphia in 1911 and fight until 1925.

During the Great Depression, he will operate a food kitchen for the homeless there. Wills will remain in New Orleans and become a boxing referee after hanging up his gloves.

....

1915 A major hurricane hits New Orleans on September 29. Dubbed The Great Storm of 1915, the Category 4 storm causes flooding and widespread wind damage, including destroying the four buildings that comprise the Bayou Road School, predecessor of the Joseph Craig School in Tremé, and the campus of Leland University in the Uptown section of the city.

The first black branch of the New Orleans Public Library is dedicated on October 24 at the intersection of Phillip and Dryades streets in a building constructed with $25,000 (nearly $600,000 in 2015 dollars) in funding from the Andrew Carnegie Foundation. The Dryades Street Colored Library, which is built to house up to 10,000 books, will remain open until 1965. The building will later be purchased by the Dryades Street YMCA to house educational programs.

The Sisters of the Blessed Sacrament open a Catholic high school on the former site of Southern University on Magazine Street in uptown New Orleans. The school will be known as Xavier University Preparatory School. Starting as a co-educational institution, Xavier Prep (as it was commonly called) will become an all-girls school in 1970. When the Sisters of the Blessed Sacrament feel they can no longer support the school financially, however, they will close it in

2013. An alumni group will buy the school from the religious order and re-open it the same year as St. Katherine Drexel Preparatory School, serving grades 7-12. Katherine Drexel (1858-1955), founder of the Sisters of the Blessed Sacrament, was a wealthy white Philadelphian who devoted her life to building schools for Negroes and Native Americans, including Xavier University of Louisiana, founded in 1925. Drexel will be canonized in 2000.

Blessed Sacrament and Holy Ghost are Catholic churches opened by the Sisters of the Blessed Sacrament to serve black parishioners. Blessed Sacrament is located on property adjacent to the order's Xavier University Preparatory School. Holy Ghost is built on Louisiana Avenue at Danneel Street. In the wake of the flooding and depopulation of New Orleans in 2005, the Archdiocese of New Orleans will later combine Holy Ghost and a Central City congregation, St. Francis de Sales Catholic Church, into one parish housed at the Holy Ghost site but named St. Katherine Drexel. Likewise, Blessed Sacrament and St. Joan of Arc will be combined into one parish operating out of the St. Joan of Arc site in the Carrollton section of the city.

The National Association for the Advancement of Colored People (NAACP), founded in 1909, opens a chapter in New Orleans. It is the NAACP's first branch south of Washington, DC. The United States Supreme Court had ruled that year in *Guinn v United States* that "Grandfather Clauses" denying the right to vote for the vast majority of black people in the South were unconstitutional. This gave the NAACP the impetus to begin organizing and advocating for black rights in the Deep South.

Violinist Armand J. Piron (1988-1943) and pianist Clarence Williams (1898-1965) launch the Piron and Williams Publishing Company. In their first year of business, they publish Piron's composition *I Wish That I Could Shimmy like My Sister Kate*, the biggest hit of his career.

The Jelly Roll Blues, composed by New Orleans piano professor Ferdinand "Jelly Roll" Morton, is published by Will Rossiter, a Chicago-based music publisher. Although the tune is described as a fox-trot at the time, it will be considered the first jazz song ever published. Morton will later record the song in 1924 as a solo piece and again in 1926 with his band, the Red Hot Peppers.

According to an oft-told tale of early attempts to record New Orleans jazz, a spokesman from the Victor Talking Machine Company approached trumpeter Freddie Keppard and his Original Creole Orchestra in December 1915 about recording their music. But first, the business man explained to the musicians, they would have to try a test recording to see if the microphones could pick up the sound of the band's bass player. Keppard turned them down, insulted that the man was asking them to audition without pay. His clarinetist George Baquet recalled him saying, "Nothing doing, boys. We won't put our stuff on records for everybody to steal." Within two years, however, the all-white Original Dixieland Jazz Band will make what is considered the first jazz recording; it will sell over a million copies. The band's leader, Jimmy LaRocca, will later claim that blacks didn't have anything to do with creating jazz.

After 1915, no black people will be hired again for the New Orleans Police Department until 1950.

1916 Corpus Christ Catholic Church opens on Onzaga Street in the Seventh Ward of the city, then the heart of the Creole of color community. It is the fifth Catholic parish established in New Orleans exclusively for black worshippers. In 1930, Corpus Christi will move into a new Spanish colonial church building at the corner of St. Bernard Avenue and Galvez Street. The parish will grow to have 12,000 parishioners and claim to be the largest black Catholic parish in the nation before desegregation of New Orleans Catholic schools and churches begins in 1962. Corpus Christi's elementary school will also grow to have an enrollment of 1,000 students and will serve as a major feeder to the black Catholic high schools in the city--St. Mary's, Xavier Prep and St. Augustine. In the years following the flooding and depopulation of New Orleans in 2005, Corpus Christi will merge with another Seventh Ward Catholic Church, Epiphany, to form Corpus Christi-Epiphany parish, operating out of the former Corpus Christi Church on St. Bernard Avenue.

1917 Two years after the opening of the parochial Xavier University Preparatory School, McDonogh #35 becomes the first public high school for black students in the state of Louisiana--and the only one in New Orleans until 1942. Located at 625 South Rampart Street, at the corner of Girod Street, on the edge of Black Storyville, the legal prostitution district that is officially shuttered in November of 1917 (and merely driven underground thereafter), the school building had formerly served as McDonogh #13 Boys' School, an elementary school for whites only. Hurricane Betsy will damage the S. Rampart Street building in 1965 and a new facility will be built to permanently house the school in 1972 at 1331 Kerlerec Street in the Tremé section of the city. In the aftermath of Hurricane Katrina in 2005, the Federal Emergency Management Agency will allocate $54 million to construct a new college preparatory high school in the Gentilly section of the city near Bayou St. John. The Orleans Parish School Board will designate the 16-acre site for McDonogh #35 and the school will open for classes there in the 2015-2016 academic year.

Camille Nickerson (1888-1982) founds the B-Sharp Music Club to support the presentation of folk and art music of the black diaspora. A pioneering ethnomusicologist specializing in the Afro-Creole folk songs of Louisiana, Nickerson was born into a leading musical family in New Orleans. Her father, William J. Nickerson, founded the Nickerson School of Music, which would provide instruction to such future jazz greats as Jelly Roll Morton and Sweet Emma Barrett. Camille Nickerson began performing as a child pianist in the Nickerson Ladies Orchestra and as an adult will have a concert career performing as "The Louisiana Lady," featuring a repertoire of traditional Afro-Creole music as well as her own new compositions in Creole. Nickerson earned a bachelor's degree in music from the Oberlin Conservatory in 1916 before founding B-Sharp. She will serve on the faculty of Howard University from 1926-1962, earn a master's degree from Oberlin in 1932, and be a major force in the National Association of Negro Musicians, serving as president of the organization in 1935. The B-Sharp Music Club will continue operating in New Orleans long after her departure, presenting performances of Black Classical Music as well as Negro Spirituals and Afro-Creole songs.

On November 17, the U.S. government orders Storyville and Black Storyville, the city's segregated prostitution districts, to be closed. The two most notorious octoroon madams, Lulu White and Countess Willie Piazza, continue to live at their former Basin Street brothels, however. Piazza carves out a legitimate career in real estate and will leave two commercial properties, jewelry and a fancy automobile when she dies in 1932. White, on the other hand, keeps getting herself arrested for selling illegal alcohol and operating houses of prostitution that mask themselves as a transient hotel, in one instance, and a soft-drink company in another. She serves time briefly at a federal penitentiary in 1919 but is released after three and a half months due to poor health. She will not die, however, until August 1931.

1918 Black women organize a Colored Domestic Union comprised of "laundresses, cooks, maids and nurse-girls." The effort is led by Ella Peete, whose husband Sylvester Peete is head of the Terminal Freight Handlers Union. Representing roughly 300 members, the union demands "fair wages and reasonable hours" for the workers. It will reach a settlement with local employers without having to call a strike. And for far too many years afterward, $1 a day and streetcar/bus fare will become the standard wage for domestics.

1919 Gilbert Academy moves to New Orleans and enters a collaborative arrangement with New Orleans University, becoming its college preparatory high school. Founded in 1870 in Franklin, LA, Gilbert Academy was a private educational institution operated by the Methodist Church. When the school moves to New Orleans, it shares a four-acre site in the 5300 block of St. Charles Avenue with New Orleans University, which will merge with Straight University in 1935 to form Dillard University and relocate to a campus in the Gentilly section of the city. This will leave the entire St. Charles Avenue campus to Gilbert, making it one of the best-equipped high schools in the nation. The Academy's grounds include its Main Building, a three-story structure built in 1886 that houses classrooms, laboratories, health clinics, an auditorium, and a 5,000-volume library. The Gilbert campus also includes a football field, basketball, tennis, and volleyball courts as well as Peck Hall, the boarding home for out-of-town girls, and the Gould mansion, an antebellum home used by school officials. Some of Gilbert's outstanding alumni will include civil rights activist and former United Nations Ambassador Andrew Young, writer Margaret Walker and Olympic sprinter Audrey Patterson. In 1949, the Methodist Church will decide to withdraw its support for Gilbert and the school is forced to close. The highly desirable real estate in the Uptown section of the city is then sold to the Archdiocese of New Orleans, which razes the buildings on the former Gilbert campus and builds a new Catholic high school for white boys.

1920 The total population of New Orleans is 387,219, according to the census: 100,930 Negro (26%), 285,916 White (74%) and 373 Other (.09%).

The New Orleans Black Pelicans, the most successful black professional baseball team in the history of New Orleans, plays in the Southern Negro League and finishes in second place. The Black Pelicans took their name from the whites-only New Orleans Pelicans, which evolved into a professional minor league baseball team after its founding as an amateur club in 1865. The Black Pelicans play in the same stadium as the Pelicans and are owned by businessman Arnold Moss (1869-1931). The Black Pelicans are one of several professional or semi-professional teams that are launched at one time or another between the 1860s and the 1940s. One of the earliest teams is the New Orleans Pinchbacks, named after the first black governor of Louisiana. The Pinchbacks declare themselves the "colored national champions" in 1888 after a successful campaign besting competition throughout the Midwest. Locally, they compete against other local black teams with names like the Cohens, the Dumonts and the Unions. These squads will be succeeded by such 20th century teams as the New Orleans Crescent Stars, which will win the Negro Southern League championship in 1933, and the similarly-named New Orleans Stars, which will relocate to the Crescent City from St. Louis for the 1940 and 1941 seasons. The Stars are members of the Negro American League, a major professional baseball organization. The Black Pelicans will continue playing into the 1940s but after Jackie Robinson becomes the first black player in modern professional baseball in 1946, black professional baseball will go into decline and the last teams and leagues will fold in the early 1960s. The Pelican nickname will be revived in 2013 by the New Orleans franchise in the National Basketball Association.

Florestine Perrault Collins (1895-1988) opens a photography studio on Rampart Street that will stay in business until 1949, when she migrates to southern California. Collins, who learned photographic techniques while passing for white, is believed to be the first black woman to own and operate a portrait studio on her own, and not as a partner with a husband, other family member or associate. Other significant New Orleans photographers from this period include Arthur P. Bedou (1882-1966), whose clients included the Sisters of the Holy Family and Xavier University, and Villard Paddio (c. 1894-1947), whose images will grace the 28-page *Crescent City Pictorial: A Souvenir Dedicated to the Progress of the Colored Citizens of New Orleans, Louisiana, America's Most Interesting City*, to be published by O.C.W. Taylor in 1926.

1922 Louis Armstrong (1901-1971) leaves New Orleans on August 8 on a train bound for Chicago. There he will begin to blossom into a preeminent jazz musician/entertainer and the best-known son of the Crescent City. His complex image as grinning coon and innovative trumpeter/vocalist from a lower-class background will make him both beloved and besmirched in the black community throughout his career. He will never again live in New Orleans after this date.

Mother Catherine Seals (1887-1930) founds the Church of the Innocent Blood in the Lower Ninth Ward section of the city. It will be a leading force in the Spiritualist movement of the 20th century, developing more than 10,000 followers--both blacks and whites. Known for her abilities to heal the sick and infirm, Mother Catherine's temple and compound will occupy an entire block before her passing and will provide housing for the needy and those being treated by the spiritualist.

Alexander Pierre Tureaud Sr. (1899-1972) joins the New Orleans Branch of the National Association for the Advancement of Colored People (NAACP), the organization he will serve for the rest of his life. A.P. Tureaud will become the most important civil rights attorney in the history of New Orleans and Louisiana, handling more than 60 cases that result in the desegregation of public schools and universities in the state, equal pay for black teachers, the abolition of whites-only elections and other critical matters. Mild-mannered and pale enough to pass for white, Tureaud will be the only regularly practicing black attorney in Louisiana between 1938 and 1947. He actively encourages and mentors the second generation of New Orleans civil rights attorneys, including Ernest Morial and Revius Ortique, who will take a more brash and combative approach to dealing with racists and racism than Tureaud. In Tureaud's heyday, of course, lynchings and assassinations of outspoken blacks were much more common in Louisiana than they would be in the 1950s and 1960s, the era of massive white resistance to black progress. In 2006, Tureaud's former home at 3121 Pauger Street will be listed on the National Register of Historic Places.

....

1923 Sidney Bechet (1897-1959), a musical prodigy who will begin leaving New Orleans in 1914 to play performances in various kinds of ensembles, records his very first sessions on July 30 under the leadership of pianist/composer/publisher Clarence Williams, another Louisiana expatriate, in New York. Bechet, who will later be recognized as the first great jazz saxophonist (he pioneered the soprano sax in jazz) and the musical equal to Louis Armstrong, records two blues numbers on this date. Later that same year, he and Armstrong record together as part of the Clarence Williams Blues Five. In 1950, Bechet will move to France and spend the rest of his life there, lionized as the great artist he was. Like Armstrong, he will always be branded a son of New Orleans, no matter where he goes.

1924 Walter L. Cohen Sr. (1860-1930) is appointed to the newly-created post of controller of the Port of New Orleans by President Calvin Coolidge. Cohen, born to a Jewish father and a free black mother, is a long-time Republican Party stalwart. His appointment is rejected three times by the Senate due to the objections of white southerners. Even after the struggle to win confirmation, Coolidge's successor, Herbert Hoover, will abolish the position in 1929, though Cohen is allowed to remain in office until his death the following year. Perhaps the highlight of Cohen's tenure as controller of the port comes in 1925 when, despite constant attacks by his enemies, he is fully exonerated by a jury on a charge of accepting bribes to permit the smuggling of liquor through the port of New Orleans.

1925 The *Louisiana Weekly* begins publishing news and opinions by and about the African American community. It is founded by editor O.C.W. (Orlando Capitola Ward) Taylor (1891-1979), an educator and future broadcast journalist, and publisher Constant C. Dejoie Sr. (1881-1970), president of Unity Industrial Life Insurance Company, whose agents are tasked with selling subscriptions to the paper, generating

4,500 by the end of October 1925, according to the *Weekly*'s own report. The newspaper begins publishing on September 19 as the *New Orleans Herald* before settling in as the *Louisiana Weekly* two issues later. After Taylor leaves the publication in 1927, Dejoie and his heirs will continue publishing the paper.

The Colored Educational Alliance of New Orleans is formed by several leaders in the local African-American community. The group's purpose is to alleviate the overcrowding of black public schools and to ensure that sufficient funding is allocated by the school board for funding and repair of black schools. Two years later, the group's efforts will begin to pay off.

1927 A new annex building for the Thomy Lafon School opens at the intersection of Sixth and S. Robertson streets in the Central City section of New Orleans, the result of organized petitioning and negotiation by local black leaders. The addition to the Lafon School accommodates 2,700 students and is described in the local press as "the largest educational building" in New Orleans and "one of the largest and finest public schools for negroes in the country."

Marcus Garvey, founder of the Universal Negro Improvement Association (UNIA), which claimed in 1920 to have four million members, is deported back to his native Jamaica from the Port of New Orleans on December 2. Considered the most powerful revolutionary black leader of his era, Garvey was convicted in June 1923 of mail fraud in connection with sales of stock in the UNIA Black Star steamship line. He began serving his five-year sentence in the Atlanta Federal Penitentiary in February 1925 before having his sentence commuted by President Calvin Coolidge in November 1927. New Orleans has one of the larger UNIA chapters in the country and more than 5,000 people come to witness Garvey's farewell address from the deck of the ship deporting him back to Jamaica.

1928 The Federation of Civic Leagues of the City of New Orleans is founded on November 28. It creates an overarching body to coordinate the activities of black civic associations based in various wards of the city. The Seventh Ward League had been the first of these organizations. Founded a year earlier in 1927, the organization quickly achieves success in getting local government to repair streets, improve drainage, install street lights, and build a school in their ward. Other neighborhoods in the city soon follow suit and the groups share their strategies and tactics with each other.

1930 The total population of New Orleans is 458,762, according to the census: 129,632 Negro (28.3%), 328,446 White (71.6%) and 684 Other (.1%).

The Municipal Auditorium, built for $2 million ($27.3 million in 2015 dollars) and having the capacity to hold over 7,800 people, opens on May 30 on the site of the former Tremé Market and part of historic Congo Square. Black people are not permitted to use the facility for many years, despite living in neighborhoods adjacent to the auditorium. Black activists will finally devise schemes to integrate the facility in 1953, however. In the 1960s, in the name of urban renewal, what will end up being called Louis Armstrong Park results in the acquisition of 32 acres adjacent to the Municipal Auditorium and the demolition of 512 buildings, precipitating the removal of hundreds of predominantly black residents and several cultural landmarks.

....

1932 Flint-Goodridge Hospital of Dillard University opens on Louisiana Avenue in uptown New Orleans. Named in honor of two white donors, the well-equipped hospital is designed to meet the medical needs of black New Orleanians and to serve as a teaching hospital for black physicians and nurses. New Orleans has 35 licensed Black doctors in 1932 but Flint-Goodridge is the only hospital in New Orleans where they can practice. Rivers Frederick (1874-1954), who will leave an estate valued at $1.5 million ($13 million in 2015 dollars) when he dies, serves as chief of surgery at Flint-Goodridge until his retirement in 1950. Albert W. Dent (1904-1984), a Georgia native, is named superintendent of the new 88-bed hospital, which is constructed at a cost of $500,000 ($8 million in 2015 dollars). He will become renowned for creating a "Penny-a-Day" insurance plan that entitles the insured to 21 days of care at Flint-Goodridge for $3.65 in annual payments. Dent will be named third president of Dillard University in 1941, a post he will occupy until retiring in 1969.

1933 Ferdinand Rousseve (1904-1965) becomes the first black licensed architect in Louisiana. Rousseve had earned degrees from the Massachusetts Institute of Technology, the University of Chicago, and Harvard, where he received his Ph.D. in architecture. He will teach at Howard, Southern and Xavier universities. He also will design churches, businesses and residential structures that are built across the South.

1937 Xavier University Press publishes *The Negro in Louisiana: Aspects of His History and His Literature* by Charles B. Rousseve (1903-1993), one of the path-breaking works of black history written by an Afro-Orleanian. Rousseve, who also wrote poetry and played music, earned a master's degree in History at Xavier and worked for 45 years in the Orleans Parish Public Schools system as an educator and administrator. He was a brother of architect Ferdinand Rousseve and six other accomplished siblings.

Obstretician and gynecologist Thelma Coffey Boutte (1911-1991), a 1934 graduate of Meharry Medical College in Nashville, interns at Flint-Goodridge Hospital and becomes the second black woman to practice medicine in New Orleans--after Ella Prescott (1876-1925)--and the first to do so for the remainder of her career.

Roosevelt Taylor (1937-) is born on July 4. He will later attend Carver High School before playing on the Grambling College Southwestern Athletic Conference 1960 champion football team. After Grambling, Taylor will go on to star as a safety with the 1963 Chicago Bears, National Football League Champions. Taylor will be selected All-Pro twice in his career and will play in the NFL from 1961-1972. He was New Orleans' first NFL superstar and unlike Louis Armstrong, who only claimed to be born on the Fourth of July, Rosey Taylor was an actual Independence Day baby.

....

1939 Edgar "Dooky" Chase Sr. and his wife Emily open a sandwich shop and lottery ticket outlet that will expand into a bar and Dooky Chase's Restaurant in 1941. In 1946, Dooky Jr. (1928-), a big band leader and concert producer, will marry the vivacious Leah Lange (1923-). She will eventually become the head chef and enlarge the restaurant's menu with classic Creole dishes, transforming Dooky Chase's into a sit-down, fine dining restaurant as well as a take-out spot with check-cashing services for working men and women. Leah, the award-winning Queen of Creole Cuisine, and Dooky Jr. will also turn the walls of their business in the 2300 block of Orleans Avenue into an exhibition space for their collection of African-American art. And in the 1950s and 1960s, when the offices of the local NAACP and Urban League are just a few blocks away, Dooky's frequently hosts gatherings of civil rights groups, especially when visiting dignitaries are in town. The restaurant is now a must-eat place for tourists and locals alike.

The Dew Drop Inn opens at 2836 LaSalle Street. Owned by Frank Painia (1911-1972), the business includes a restaurant, bar, barbershop, hotel and night club that features shows with a variety of entertainment--singers, exotic dancers, female impersonators, comedians and other acts. The Dew Drop, which bills itself as "the South's swankiest night club," becomes both a spawning ground for local rhythm & blues musicians and a showcase for emerging and established touring artists. The club soon achieves legendary status for its late night jam sessions and its house bands as well as its floor shows and amateur nights. Everybody who is somebody makes their way there. With integration in the mid-1960s, however, business slacks off and the night club is all but defunct by the time Painia dies in the early 1970s. Other black-owned clubs like Prout's, Mason's, Sylvia's, Del's and the Nightcap soldier on for a few more years, but they too succumb to market forces as more and more black entertainers and patrons flock to white-owned venues in the French Quarter and other sections of town.

1940 The total population of New Orleans is 494,537, according to the census: 149,034 Negro (30.1%), 344,775 White (69.8%) and 728 Other (.1%).

The *New Orleans Sentinel* begins publication as a weekly newspaper. It is founded by a collection of young, progressive-minded working-class activists within the local NAACP chapter who call themselves The Group. They had attempted to wrest control of the organization the year before but had lost the election. The leaders are postal service workers Donald Jones and John E. Rousseau Jr., who edits the paper, and

Arthur J. Chapital, who will later serve as president of the New Orleans NAACP from 1952-1962 and expand chapter membership four-fold to 3,000. In the mid-1940s, the *Sentinel* will merge with publisher Carter Wesley's *Houston Informer* and become the *New Orleans Informer and Sentinel.* Rousseau (1909-2001) also will go on to edit the Louisiana version of the *Pittsburgh Courier* and the *Louisiana Weekly.* One of his best efforts as a journalist will be investigating and doggedly publicizing the case of Edgar Labat and Clifton Poret, two African-American men wrongfully convicted by an all-white jury for the 1950 rape of a white woman in New Orleans. Both men will be sentenced to the death penalty in 1953 and suffer through nine stays of execution. They will ultimately win their release in 1967 but not without the distinction of being the longest serving death row inmates in modern U.S. history at the time.

Prestigious New York publisher Houghton Mifflin issues the *New Orleans Cook Book* by culinary pioneer Lena Richard (1892?-1950). She will also become the first woman in the South to be featured in her own 15-minute television program when "Lena Richard's New Orleans Cook Book" airs twice-weekly--generally at 5 PM on Tuesdays and Thursdays--on WDSU-TV in 1949-1950. Born Lena Paul in New Roads, Louisiana, she moved to New Orleans as a young girl with her family. Starting out as a domestic worker, she trained at several cooking schools in New Orleans (with the support of her wealthy white employers/patrons) and in 1918 graduated from the Fannie

Farmer Cooking School in Boston. After years of operating food establishments and a catering service, Richard launched her own cooking school in 1937. In 1939, she publishes *Lena Richard's Cook Book*, which Houghton Mifflin reissues the following year under a new title. The publication leads to opportunities for Richard to serve as chef at establishments in New York state and Colonial Williamsburg in Virginia. Returning to New Orleans in 1945, she will launch a line of frozen dinners that are distributed across the country. In 1949, she will open her most well-known eatery, Lena Richard's Gumbo House, at the corner of Louisiana Avenue and Danneel Street. After she dies the following year, Percival Richard, her widower, and other family members will keep the business going until 1958. The Gumbo House will later be immortalized in the 1969 scatological, underground-classic novel *Groove, Bang and Jive Around* by New Orleans native Steve Cannon.

1941 The Magnolia housing project opens in the Central City neighborhood. New Orleans is the first city in the nation to construct public housing under the authority of the federal Wagner Act, which is intended to eliminate slums and replace them with higher-quality housing. New Orleans will eventually end up with more than 10,000 public housing units by the 1960s. The properties will house increasing percentages of black residents, including even those initially built for white residents only, and the city will rank second in the nation at one point in the percentage of its residents living in public housing. Through lack of maintenance and demolition, however, the number of units will begin to steadily decline through the end of the 20th century. In 2007, using the damage wrought by Hurricane Katrina as an excuse, the New Orleans City Council will vote to demolish the last 3,077 remaining public housing units and to replace them with mixed-income developments owned and managed by private companies.

The People's Defense League (PDL) is founded by Ernest J. Wright (1909-1979), a civil rights activist and organizer. The Federal Bureau of Investigation will later characterize it as "the most powerful negro organization in New Orleans." Wright was educated at Xavier University of Louisiana and the University of Michigan in the 1930s. He also writes a weekly column for the *Louisiana Weekly*. The PDL will work to combat police brutality and racial discrimination, to advocate for the unionization of black workers and the right-to-vote for black citizens. The organization emerges after a strike in September 1940 by black insurance agents after the black-owned companies they worked for--the most potent economic force in the black community at that time--quashed their attempts to form a labor union. The situation turns nasty when the companies hires new agents to replace the strikers and has them protected by private security forces. The strikers and their supporters then arm themselves. There is a confrontation on October 8. Ernest Wright and five others are arrested and charged with assault with a deadly weapon. Wright serves a 60-day sentence and while he is jailed the insurance owners break the strike. Nevertheless, there is a cheering crowd to greet him when he leaves jail in November. He is soon hired by the Congress of Industrial Organizations (CIO), a federation of labor unions, and later helps organize 3,000 laundry workers.

1942 Booker T. Washington High School opens as only the second public high school for blacks in New Orleans. Located at 1201 South Roman Street, adjacent to the old Calliope Housing Project, both the school and the public housing complex were built on the site of the former Clio Street/Silver City dump site, which was closed in the 1930s. In addition to a college preparatory curriculum, Washington High stresses an industrial and manual arts education program. At its opening, the school enrolls 1,600 students. Its 1,700-seat auditorium is the major performance venue for touring black artists like Paul Robeson and the Duke Ellington Orchestra in the 1940s and 1950s. After years of declining enrollment in the 1990s, the school will be shuttered after Hurricane Katrina in 2005. The federal government will then allocate $55 million for a new facility to be constructed on the site. The old structure, except for the auditorium, will be demolished and the new facility, scheduled to open in 2017, will be assigned to a white-led charter school management corporation, New Orleans College Prep.

1943 Reverend Abraham Lincoln Davis (1914-1978), pastor of the large and well-established New Zion Baptist Church, and activist/organizer Ernest J. Wright launch the Louisiana Association for the Progress of

Negro Citizens, which works to secure the vote for black citizens. Though there are roughly 150,000 black residents in the city at the time, only 400 are registered to vote. Davis is an early proponent of what will later come to be called liberation theology; he believes the church has an obligation to fight for the rights of its oppressed citizens. Davis will go on to found the Orleans Parish Progressive Voters League (OPPVL) in 1949 and to co-found the Southern Christian Leadership Conference (SCLC) in 1957 along with Martin Luther King Jr. among others. Davis also will become a key political operative and liaison between the white political and economic establishment in New Orleans and the black community. In 1975, Davis will be appointed to the New Orleans City Council, making him the first black to hold such a position since the 1870s.

Calvin Moret (1925-2015) leaves New Orleans on December 8 and arrives in Tuskegee, Alabama, during World War II to begin training as a fighter pilot for the 332nd Fighter Group, better known as the Tuskegee Airmen. These are the first African Americans trained as fighter pilots. Nine hundred and fifty-three black men from every corner of the United States (and one from Port au Prince, Haiti) will survive the rigorous training at the Tuskegee Air Force Base for the rigorous training; 450 of them will fly over 15,000 missions during the war, earning 850 medals for their service. Sixty-six Tuskegee airmen will be killed during the war but no bomber planes they escort will ever be lost. Moret will be one of five New Orleanians trained at Tuskegee; Russell Desvignes, Walter Downs, Albert Lieteau and Haydel White are the others. Moret, who will become the last surviving Tuskegee Airman from New Orleans, never gets a chance to engage in combat after being commissioned on November 20, 1944. First Germany and then Japan surrender in 1945 before Moret sees any action. After leaving the Air Force in January 1946, Moret returns to New Orleans, joins his family's printing business and establishes the Pelican Flying Club in 1949 along with his older brother Adolph, who had learned to fly before the war, and other local black aviators.

O.C.W. Taylor (1891-1979) becomes the first black person in New Orleans to host a non-religious radio talk show when he launches a program on WNOE that runs for 22 years. In 1966, he will produce and host a 4-hour weekly television program on WWOM-TV that remains on air for two and half years.

1947 The original Roy Brown (1925-1981) version of the jump blues song *Good Rocking Tonight* is released on DeLuxe Records, based then in New Jersey. It becomes a hit in New Orleans before sparking interest around the rest of the country. Brown, who wrote the song and tried to convince the better-known Wynonie Harris to record it, was a New Orleans native who moved to the West Coast in the 1940s. His version of *Good Rocking Tonight*, later considered one of the first rock & roll songs, reaches #13 on the Billboard R&B chart. After Brown's success, Harris records the song and his version becomes a #1 R&B hit and remains on the chart for half a year. Brown's single will re-enter the chart in 1949, peaking at #11. Through the years, artists like Elvis Presley, Paul McCartney and Bruce Springsteen will also record popular versions of the song.

1948 George "Tex" Stephens becomes the first black disc jockey in New Orleans when he begins broadcasting a "race music" show on white-owned WJBW-AM radio. Stevens' program is broadcast from the Gladstone Hotel at 3435 Dryades Street because he is not allowed to work out of the station's own studio. The following year, he will move to the newly-launched WMRY, the city's first black-oriented station, which begins broadcasting from The Court of Two Sisters Restaurant in the French Quarter. Another pioneering disc jockey from this era is Vernon "Dr. Daddy-O" Winslow, who will begin hosting a black music show on WWEZ in 1949. It will be sponsored by local brewer Jax Beer.

Audrey "Mickey" Patterson (1926-1996) becomes the first African-American woman to win an Olympic medal when she places third in the 200-meter dash at the London Olympics on August 6. Patterson, who attended Gilbert Academy before running on the collegiate level for Tennessee State University, will later move to California and start her own youth track club, Mickey's Missiles.

1949 Pianist/vocalist Antoine "Fats" Domino (1928-) records "The Fat Man" for Imperial Records. By 1953 it will sell one million copies and help define the New Orleans sound in rhythm & blues and early rock and roll. Domino, working in collaboration with producer, arranger, and songwriter Dave Bartholomew (1918-), will record 37 top 40 hits by 1963. His best seller will be 1956's *Blueberry Hill*, which sells over 5 million copies.

1950 The total population of New Orleans is 570,445: 181,775 Negro (31.9%), 387,814 White (68%) and 856 Other (.1%).

Voter registration campaigns have been so successful in New Orleans that the number of black registered voters grows from 400 in 1940 to 26,000 by 1950.

After five years of focused demands, two black men are hired by the New Orleans Police Department (NOPD). They are not issued uniforms, however, and are not permitted to arrest whites.

1951 St. Augustine High School opens as an educational institution for black boys, the first school of its kind in New Orleans. Operated by the overwhelmingly white Society of St. Joseph of the Sacred Heart, St. Augustine will go on to become an academic juggernaut and an athletic powerhouse for decades. In addition, the school's band, the Marching 100, will be widely hailed as one of the nation's best. The school's leadership will eventually be turned over to African-American adults.

1952 *Bush v Orleans Parish School Board* suit is filed seeking to force the desegregation of New Orleans public schools. Filed by the local NAACP, the suit will be decided in May 1954 by the U.S. Supreme Court as part of the seven similar cases bundled in the *Brown v Kansas Board of Education* decision outlawing segregated public schools.

1953 The United Clubs, Inc. a coalition of social aid and pleasure clubs organized chiefly by physician/entrepreneur/civic leader Leonard Burns (1922-2008), integrates the New Orleans Municipal Auditorium when it rents the facility and presents a ball in support of the United Negro College Fund. Though the auditorium had been built in 1929 on the site of historic Congo Square and hundreds of black residents had been displaced in order for the project to proceed, the facility had a whites-only policy. The United Clubs group pay the full rental fee for the auditorium in advance for what they informed the facility would be a "university" event. The trick works and they rent the building again the following year for a UNCF benefit.

1954 Nearly 32,000 black public school students, along with their teachers and principals, boycott the McDonogh Day ceremony on May 7 as a protest against the racially discriminatory manner in which the event is being conducted. Every year, all New Orleans Public Schools students are brought to Lafayette Square to pay homage to the late John McDonogh, a 19th-century philanthropist who had endowed public schools in the city. Delegations from white schools place flowers at the McDonogh statue, sing songs, receive keys to the city from the mayor and leave. Delegations from black schools, meanwhile, have to wait until after all the white students have finished before having their separate ceremony afterward, often standing all the while during the white portion of the program in hot, muggy, or otherwise uncomfortable weather. When black teachers begin organizing to protest the treatment, they are backed by the local NAACP chapter and other civil rights activists. The boycott works; only 34 black students show up for the McDonogh Day ceremony that year. Ten days later, the U.S. Supreme Court issues its ruling in the *Brown v Kansas Board of Education* case outlawing segregation in public schools across the nation. Despite the official ban on segregation, however, the black community's boycott of McDonogh Day will have to be repeated in 1955.

A redesigned and modernized Lincoln Beach opens on May 8 along Lake Pontchartrain in eastern New Orleans as the finest amusement park in the South for Negroes. The attraction features a ferris wheel and other rides, a huge swimming pool, a midway, a modest man-made beach, and a space for special events such as music concerts and beauty contests. Lincoln Beach was originally provided to black patrons by the Orleans Parish Levee Board in 1939, the year after construction started on Pontchartrain Beach as a whites-only swimming and amusement facility in the previously-integrated Milneburg section of the lakefront. Lincoln Beach, located farther east in the

Little Woods area, is an appeasement to black citizens who wanted a space of their own for swimming and recreation. And though the Orleans Levee Board built a bathhouse in 1941 at the 2.3-acre Lincoln Beach site, it is paltry in comparison to the accommodations at Pontchartrain Beach. After years of further agitation by community leaders, $500,000 in renovations are made to the site and completed in 1954. However, this new and improved version of the amusement park will close in 1965 after integration of the previously all-white--and much larger--Pontchartrain Beach draws the clientele away from Lincoln Beach. Additionally, Lincoln Beach's lease, which stipulates that the facility operate to serve Negroes exclusively, is in conflict with the federal 1964 Civil Rights Act and court orders barring racially segregated public accommodations.

1955 Pontchartrain Park, located in the eastern section of New Orleans, formally opens on June 27 as the first subdivision in the city created for middle-class black families. The 200-acre neighborhood features slab-on-grade, not raised, single family homes and an 18-hole, par-72 golf course designed by Joseph Bartholomew (1885?-1971), a black New Orleanian who becomes a nationally acclaimed designer of golf courses, including many he could never play on. Pontchartrain Park was developed by white philanthropists Edgar and Edith Stern (Sears Roebuck Company heirs) and Chuck and Rosa Keller (Louisiana Coca-Cola Company heirs) as a way to demonstrate that middle-class blacks, including military veterans with access to GI loans, were creditworthy and reliable enough to borrow money for home mortgages. Pontchartrain Park contains 1,000 homes that initially sell for $10,000-$27,000. The $15 million ($131 million in 2015 dollars) development also helps relieve a shortage of housing in the then-growing city and momentarily slows the push for residential integration in other middle class neighborhoods like Lakeview and Gentilly, which had instituted deed covenants as early as 1905 forbidding sales of homes to blacks.

1956 On May 21, the $23 million ($201.5 million in 2015 dollars) Desire Housing projects open to Negro tenants only. The largest public housing development in the history of New Orleans, the Desire is comprised of 262 two-story brick-veneer buildings containing roughly 1,860 units on 98.5 acres of land in the Ninth Ward bounded by Higgins Boulevard, Alvar Street, Florida Boulevard, Desire Street, Oliver White Avenue, Pleasure Street and Piety Street. By the mid-1960s, the Desire is home to 13,000 residents, making it the densest residential area in the city. Due to the shoddy construction of the housing units, however, the property falls into a state of disrepair and many buildings become uninhabitable. Units start being demolished in 1996 and demolition continues in phases until 2003 when the last two of the original buildings are preserved for historical purposes.

1957 The Southern Christian Leadership Conference (SCLC) is founded in New Orleans at New Zion Baptist

Church, pastored by Rev. A.L. Davis, in the Central City neighborhood. Under the leadership of Martin Luther King Jr., the SCLC will grow into one of the Big Six national Civil Rights Movement organizations.

The United Clubs, Inc. stages the first Carnival Blackout. Instead of spending their money to produce balls and other activities during the Carnival season, most of the clubs pool their money and donate $60,000 to support the Civil Rights Movement in Montgomery, Alabama.

1959 International Longshoremen Association Local 1419, the largest black labor union in the United States, commissions the design and building of a modernist building at 2700 South Claiborne Avenue as its headquarters. Led by union President Clarence "Chink" Henry, the ILA Hall costs $500,000 ($4 million in 2015 dollars) to build and serves as an important community venue for decades until it will be severely damaged by Hurricane Katrina flooding in 2005 and subsequently torn down.

1960 The total population of New Orleans is 627,525, according to the census: 233,514 Negro (37.2%), 393,594 White (62.7%) and 1,417 Other (.1%). After 1960, the overall population of the city declines each decade as whites move in increasing numbers to the suburbs.

The Consumers' League, an organization founded by optometrist Dr. Henry Mitchell, educator Dr.

Raymond Floyd and future State Representative Rev. Avery Alexander (1910-1999), launches a boycott of Dryades Street, the city's second largest shopping district, after merchants there refuse to hire blacks for jobs above the menial level, as clerks, sales people and managers. The boycott is launched two weeks before Easter. It works. By mid-May, the Consumers' League claim 30 new jobs have been created for blacks in Dryades Street stores. That success leads to the formation of the Citizens' Committee (echoing the Citizens Committee of the 1890s that orchestrated the *Plessy v Ferguson* case), a coalition of black organizations that work between 1961 and 1964 to force more employment concessions out of white businesses, and the Coordinating Council of Greater New Orleans, which organizes voter-registration drives in the black community between 1961 and 1965. Among the college students who participate in the Consumers' League picket lines are Rudy Lombard, Jerome Smith and Oretha Castle, who will form a New Orleans chapter of the Congress of Racial Equality (CORE) to continue nonviolent direct-action campaigns aimed at dismantling racial segregation.

On September 9, seven members of the racially mixed CORE stage a sit-in at the lunch counter at the F.W. Woolworth's Department Store on Canal Street. They are arrested, charged with criminal mischief and bailed out later that day. The following day, the local NAACP Youth Council pickets Woolworth's in a display of solidarity with CORE. On September 12, Mayor deLesseps Morrison bans all picketing and sit-ins. CORE representatives then meet with the mayor to encourage him to have store owners open their lunch counters to black patrons. The mayor does nothing. On Friday, September 16, a CORE worker and five members of the Consumers' League picket a shopping center and are arrested; three of them are held in jail until Sunday evening. On Saturday, September 17, however, local CORE chairman Rudy Lombard, Oretha Castle, Cecil Carter, a Dillard University student, and Lanny Goldfinch, a white Tulane University student, sit-in at the lunch counter at McCrory's. They are arrested. The black activists are charged with criminal mischief and released on $250 bail. Goldfinch is charged with criminal anarchy, which carries a maximum sentence of 10 years and a $2,500 bond. The group will challenge the legality of these arrests and take their argument all the way to the U.S. Supreme Court in a case that will come to be known as *Lombard v Louisiana.*

The integration of New Orleans public schools begins on November 14 when four black girls attend the first grade at two Ninth Ward elementary schools. Six-year-old Ruby Bridges integrates William Franz Elementary School while Leona Tate, Tessie Prevost and Gail Etienne enroll in McDonogh 19. All four attend school with the protection of federal marshals who keep rabid mobs of whites at bay when the racists gather outside the schools each day attempting to keep the children out. These actions are part of a campaign of "Massive Resistance" that the white power structure throughout the South deploys in its attempts to use any means available, including terrorism, shady legal maneuverings and economic reprisals, to halt court-ordered integration. When these demonstrations fail to prevent the integration of the New Orleans public schools, white parents begin withdrawing their children from the public school system in New Orleans, creating whites-only private schools and moving to white suburban communities. By 1970, New Orleans public schools are 70% black; by 1980, black enrollment is over 95%.

Robert Collins (1931-), Nils Douglas (1930-2003), and Lolis Elie (1930-) form what ends up becoming the "most radical" black law firm in New Orleans when, despite their original plan to try to make some money, they start taking on civil rights cases and representing activists working for CORE. The firm will dissolve in 1971. In 1978, Collins will be appointed by President Jimmy Carter to a judgeship on the United States District Court of the Eastern District of Louisiana. That will make him the first black federal judge in the South. In 1991, however, he will be convicted of accepting payments to influence his sentencing of a drug smuggler and serve five years in a federal prison. After unsuccessful campaigns for legislative office in the 1960s, Douglas will be appointed Criminal District Court Commissioner for Orleans Parish in 1973, a position he will occupy until his retirement in 1986. Elie will later form a law partnership with white attorney Al Bronstein and establish a training program for young black lawyers.

1961 The United Clubs, Inc. stage a second Carnival
Blackout in 1961 that garners widespread support.
The boycott is designed to protest the racist maneuvers
of the Louisiana Legislature and the White Citizens'
Council opposing the integration of New Orleans
public schools. The most notable non-supporter of
the boycott is the Zulu Social Aid and Pleasure Club,
whose members don their usual blackface and parade
on Mardi Gras anyway.

Ernie K-Doe (Ernest Kador Jr., 1936-2001) records
the Allen Toussaint composition "Mother-in-Law"
which goes to #1 on the *Billboard* Hot 100 chart
in the U.S. This will be K-Doe's greatest recording
success. Toussaint (1938-2015) will become the most
successful composer of popular music in the city's
history.

Preservation Hall opens in the French Quarter as
a showcase for traditional New Orleans jazz, which
has been waning in popularity for more than 30
years. The proprietors are two young Jews from
Pennsylvania, Allan and Sandra Jaffe. The audiences
at the venue are predominantly white; the musicians
are predominantly black, old, docile, if not doddering,
and generally from the first or second generation of
New Orleans jazz innovators. In a few short years, The
Preservation Hall Jazz Band is not only performing
nightly in New Orleans for tourists and locals, there is
also a touring unit playing festivals and concert halls
around the world.

In May, the national office of CORE begins Freedom Rides on Greyhounds and Trailways buses to test a Supreme Court ban on discrimination on interstate carriers. CORE had planned to send interracial groups of testers to travel from Washington, DC to New Orleans, integrating facilities and amenities at stations along the way. When the first group reaches Alabama, however, a group of riders is badly beaten by white mobs in Birmingham and one of the buses is attacked and burned in Anniston. Determined to keep the rides going, the national office requests volunteers from the New Orleans chapter go to Montgomery and continue the rides from there. Five New Orleanians volunteer--Doris Jean Castle, Jean Thompson, Julia Aaron, Dave Dennis and Jerome Smith. When their bus reaches Jackson, MS, the riders are arrested. Castle and Aaron refuse bail and end up serving 60 days in Mississippi's notorious Parchman Prison. A worse fate befalls Jerome Smith. In McComb, MS, he is beaten so badly his skull gets cracked and he will need operations to insert and secure a metal plate in his head. Despite his injuries, Smith returns to Mississippi when he is well enough and works as an organizer there until returning to New Orleans in 1966.

Musicians Harold Battiste Jr., John Boudreaux, Peter "Chuck" Badie, Roy Montrell and Red Tyler form All For One (AFO) Records in May of this year. One of their first recordings is *I Know (You Don't Love Me No More)* featuring a young vocalist named Barbara George. It turns out to be a major hit, reaching #1 on the R&B

charts and #3 on the pop charts that year. While the pioneering artist-owned label will never enjoy that level of commercial success and visibility again, Battiste (1931-2015) will continue guiding it through fits and starts to produce significant New Orleans jazz and R&B recordings into the 21st century.

1962 Catholic schools in New Orleans integrate peaceably but Afro-Orleanians do not abandon the traditional black Catholic schools in large numbers.

Fifteen white-owned Canal Street stores peacefully desegregate their lunch counters on September 15 as a result of negotiations conducted by the Citizens' Committee with local white business leaders. Nevertheless, the NAACP Youth Council will continue to picket outside several of these stores until 1965.

1963 In February, 11 black students register for classes at Tulane University, the city's largest private university. Pearlie Hardin Elloie and Barbara Marie Guillory had filed suit in 1961 in federal court seeking admittance to Tulane's graduate school. In December 1962, the court ruled that the school could voluntarily admit Negro students without jeopardizing its status as a private institution. In 1882, when Paul Tulane made his bequest to the university that would come to bear his name, he stipulated that the funds be used for "the promotion and encouragement of intellectual, moral and industrial education among the white young persons in the city of New Orleans, State of Louisiana." In 1961, prior to the lawsuit, the university's board approved a policy permitting the school to "admit qualified students regardless of race or color if it were legally permissible." Tulane's integration proceeds relatively peaceably.

On May 20, the U.S. Supreme Court rules that the City of New Orleans' attempt to ban peaceful sit-ins is unconstitutional, essentially paving the way for the desegregation of lunch counters and other public places. The case, *Lombard v Louisiana*, grew out of the arrest of Rudy Lombard (1939-2014) and other members of CORE on September 17, 1960, when they defied a proclamation by then-Mayor deLesseps Morrison outlawing sit-ins in New Orleans. The case was handled initially by the New Orleans black law firm, Collins, Douglas and Elie, and argued all the way to the U.S. Supreme Court by white attorney Jack Nelson after being denied relief at the state level.

On September 30, the largest civil rights demonstration in New Orleans history is held one month after the national March on Washington. More than 10,000 blacks and 300 whites trek from Shakspeare (sic) Park to City Hall in the Freedom March to present demands to the local government to provide more employment opportunities and political participation to black people, to desegregate all public accommodations in the city and to stop police brutality of black citizens. The march is led by the Interdenominational Ministerial Alliance (headed by A.L. Davis, Avery Alexander and Milton Upton), the NAACP (Ernest Morial and A.J. Chapital) and CORE (Oretha Castle).

Members of CORE and Rev. Avery Alexander sit-in at the City Hall Cafeteria on Halloween in an attempt to integrate it. When the demonstrators refuse to move, police officers forcibly carry them out of the building. Alexander is dragged out feet-first down the stone steps of City Hall.

1964 CORE pickets the Loew's Theater on Canal Street, objecting to its segregated seating arrangements until the federal Civil Rights Act is enacted on July 2. The law bans discrimination in public accommodations, the workplace, schools and voter registration processes. It is a decisive victory for the Civil Rights Movement in New Orleans and the South.

The Free Southern Theater, founded in 1963 at Tougaloo College by Doris Derby (1940-), Gilbert Moses (1942-1995), and John O'Neal (1940-), moves to New Orleans in September and continues to perform in rural communities throughout the Deep South in its role as the cultural wing of the Student Nonviolent Coordinating Committee. The organization will become an all-black company later in the 1960s and will serve as the epicenter of the Black Arts Movement in New Orleans under the stewardship of Tom Dent (1932-1998) and Vallery Ferdinand III (Kalamu ya Salaam) (1947-) before collapsing in 1978.

Theron "T-Bird" Lewis, who will set the 440-yard indoor world record in 1967, is an alternate member of the gold medal-winning 4x400 meter relay team for the United States in the 1964 Toyko Olympics.

Though Lewis, who prepped at Carver High, doesn't get the opportunity to run in the finals on October 21, he is the second black from New Orleans to earn a spot on an Olympics squad. In 1966, he will be part of the first 4x400 relay team to run the race in under three minutes. Lewis will also be a three-time All-America sprinter at Southern University from 1965-1967.

The Dixie Cups reach the #1 spot on the Billboard charts for three weeks with their recording of "Chapel of Love" written by non-Orleanians Phil Spector, Jeff Barrie and Ellie Greenwich. The million-seller, which is also their first recording, will be the group's biggest hit. The trio is comprised of sisters Barbara Ann and Rosa Lee Hawkins and their cousin Joan Marie Johnson, all reared in the Calliope housing projects. After a string of successful releases in 1964 and 1965, the group's production and success will tail off as waves of British artists like The Beatles and the Rolling Stones begin to dominate American music sales.

1965 Harold Perry (1916-1991), a native of Lake Charles, LA, is appointed auxiliary bishop of the Archdiocese of New Orleans by Pope Paul VI on September 29. He is the first African American of the modern era to become a Catholic bishop. At his ordination ceremony on January 6, 1966, white protestors hold a demonstration outside the church; one woman calls Perry's appointment "another reason why God will destroy the Vatican." As an auxiliary bishop, Perry serves as pastor of Our Lady of Lourdes Church and

St. Theresa of the Child Jesus Church in New Orleans, vicar general (second in command) of the archdiocese, and rector (managerial and spiritual head) of the National Shrine of Our Lady of Prompt Succor. He lives on the grounds of Ursuline Academy, the oldest girl's school in the United States. For many years he also serves as national chaplain of the Knights of Peter Claver, the nation's largest black Catholic service organization. Perry will die at age 74 due to complications of Alzheimer's disease.

On September 9, Hurricane Betsy comes ashore at Grand Isle, LA, as a Category 3 storm packing winds up to 145 miles per hour. It destroys communities in St. Bernard and Plaquemines parishes. The Lower Ninth Ward is flooded and many of the black residents there are displaced by what was then the most destructive storm in Louisiana history -- $1.2 billion ($9 billion in 2015 dollars) in property damage.

George Oliver Mondy Jr. (1938-1996) becomes the first black employee of the New Orleans Fire Department. He will retire in 1991 and become an ordained minister the following year. Mondy, a graduate of McDonogh #35 High School and a former drill sergeant in the U.S. Marine Corps, will be one of the founders of the Black Association of New Orleans Firefighters.

1966 Attorneys Robert Collins, Nils Douglas and Lolis Elie found the Southern Organization for Unified Leadership (SOUL), which registers black voters and becomes a leading force in electoral politics in

New Orleans. The federal Voting Rights Act of 1965 had stripped away many of the barriers that racist regimes in the South deployed to keep large numbers of black people from becoming registered to vote. In 1963, local black leaders estimated that there were 125,000 eligible black voters in New Orleans but only 36,000 were actually registered. By 1966, there are 66,000 black voters on the rolls, thanks in large measure to the unrelenting voter registration drives of the Coordinating Council of Greater New Orleans (CCGNO), a coalition of black civic and political organizations. This increase in voting strength permits black candidates to successfully vie for elective office while forcing white candidates who need black support to address the needs of the black community. SOUL's success will lead Robert Collins to found another black political organization in 1969, COUP (Community Organization for Urban Politics), which in turn leads to the formation of other groups such as BOLD (Black Organization for Leadership Development) and LIFE (Louisiana Independent Federation of Electors).

CORE shuts down operations in New Orleans. After the notoriety of the Freedom Rides, the local CORE chapter membership mushroomed to more than 300, a majority of whom were white college students. Tensions soon began rising, however, between the chapter's black and white members. The black leadership, headed by Oretha Castle, claims the organization has become known as a place white men can have easy access to black women and that several of the whites keep attempting to usurp leadership of the chapter. So, they expel all the whites. The national office objects and later some whites are allowed back in but the racial tension never completely dies down. At the 1965 national CORE meeting, New Orleanian Matt Suarez and several others support a resolution opposing the Vietnam War. When the national leadership has the measure tabled, he and more than a dozen others immediately resign from the organization. As many as 15 more members in New Orleans leave over the next two months. When the national office cuts the budget for the New Orleans field offices in 1965 at the seeming expense of expanding personnel and operations in New York, the New Orleans leaders move on to other pursuits. By this point, the battle for desegregation has been won--by law, at least.

Singer Aaron Neville (1941-) hits #1 on Billboard's R&B Chart and #2 on the Hot 100 with "Tell It Like It Is." Neville will later be part of a triple platinum project when he duets with Linda Rondstadt in 1989 on her *Cry Like a Rainstorm, Howl Like the Wind* album that sells 3 million copies. He will also join brothers Art, Charles and Cyril in the 1970s to form cult favorites The Neville Brothers. They will follow in the footsteps of Bo Dollis and the Wild Magnolias to expand the integration of Mardi Gras/Black Indian chants and rhythms into contemporary funk and help brand another phase of New Orleans musical innovation.

New Orleans *Data News Weekly*, founded by veteran black journalist Joseph "Scoop" Jones, begins publication as "The People's Paper."

....

1967 On February 2, the New Orleans Buccaneers become a charter member of the American Basketball Association (ABA). Jimmy Jones, a guard who played collegiately at Grambling College, is a starter on the team, making him the city's first black professional basketball star. The Bucs will play three seasons in New Orleans before being sold in August 1970 and moved to Memphis. The ABA itself lasts nine seasons. In 1974, the city will be awarded a franchise in the National Basketball Association, the New Orleans Jazz. That team will stay for five seasons before moving to Utah. In 2002, the Charlotte Hornets franchise will move to New Orleans. After a change in ownership, the team will be renamed the New Orleans Pelicans in 2013.

Marlbert "Spider" Pradd (1944-2014), a 6'3", 170-pound shooting guard, finishes his career at Dillard University with a 37.5 point scoring average. A Chicago native, Pradd is the most prolific scorer in New Orleans collegiate basketball history. He will play for two seasons with the New Orleans Buccaneers in the American Basketball Association as a little-used reserve. Pradd continues to live in New Orleans after his stint in the pros. He will be elected to the Louisiana Basketball Hall of Fame in 2003.

On the very first play of the first regular season game played by the New Orleans Saints in the National Football League (NFL) on September 17, wide receiver John Gilliam returns the opening kickoff 94 yards for a touchdown at Tulane University Stadium before a crowd of nearly 81,000. Despite the promising start, the Saints will lose the game and have losing seasons until 1987. In 2010, the team will reach the pinnacle of its sport when it wins Super Bowl 44. Like most teams in the NFL, a majority of the Saints players will be black by this time. The city would never have been awarded an NFL franchise, or any other major professional sports franchise, for that matter, if it had not stopped most of its overtly segregationist practices against black people in the 1960s.

1968 Construction is completed on the North Claiborne Avenue overpass portion of Interstate-10. Like much of the rest of the federal highway system built after World War II, the highway project, begun in 1961, is intentionally routed through the heart of an historic, economically vibrant black community, virtually destroying it. Along an eight-block stretch of the formerly oak-lined avenue impacted by the overpass, the number of businesses--many of them black-owned--declines from 132 in 1960 to 35 in 2000.

Civil Rights Movement veteran Jerome Smith (1939-) founds Tamborine (sic) and Fan, which will develop into a renowned youth development organization modeled on the Freedom Schools of the mid-1960s with the additional element of teaching and passing on New Orleans grassroots cultural traditions like second-lining.

....

1970 The total population of New Orleans is 593,471, according to the census: 267,308 Negro (45%), 323,420 White (54.5%) and 2,743 Other (.5%).

Maurice "Moon" Landrieu (1930-), a white politician, begins the first of two four-year terms as mayor of New Orleans. He had been elected the previous fall with a large percentage of the black vote. During his administration, black employment at City Hall will increase from 10% to 40% of the workforce.

The *Black Collegian Magazine* is founded in New Orleans by a collective of eight twenty-something men and women with Preston Edwards Sr. serving as publisher. In response to the waves of unrest spreading to campuses across the country, the magazine's founders seek to create a communications vehicle for black college students at historically black colleges and universities as well as historically white schools. At its peak in the mid-1980s, the bi-monthly *Black Collegian Magazine* will be distributed on over 1400 campuses and grow to have a readership of 250,000. In addition to cultural information and political insight, its focus will be providing career advice and employment leads to students, especially those in science and engineering fields. After a significant slide in readership beginning in the 1990s, the publication will be rebranded in 2011 as *Diversity Employers Magazine.*

On September 15, officers from the New Orleans Police Department (NOPD) exchange gunfire with members of the New Orleans chapter of the Black Panther Party at the Panthers' headquarters on Piety Street in the city's Lower Ninth Ward. No deaths result from the shootings but 12 Black Panthers are arrested for murder charges. They are later found not guilty by an all-white jury. Well before that trial and verdict, however, the organization gets evicted from its headquarters by the property's landlord and relocated to the Desire Housing Project building #3315. On November 19, the NOPD raids the Black Panther headquarters in attempts to oust them. NOPD brass send in 250 armed cops backed by a tank and helicopters. No one is killed, however, and no shots are fired; Desire residents, many of them children, surround the Panther apartment and stay there until the police are ordered back to their buses and leave. On November 26, however, the NOPD returns, disguised this time as priests and postal workers. They charge the apartment, shooting Black Panther Betty Powell in the shoulder as she tries to slam the door on them. All six Black Panthers inside are arrested and charged with attempted murder and violation of the Federal Firearms Act. They, too, will all be eventually acquitted.

1971 Dorothy Mae Taylor (1928-2000) becomes the first black woman elected to the Louisiana Legislature on

November 6. Activist Oretha Castle Haley serves as her campaign manager. Taylor will serve in the Legislature until 1980. She will later be elected as an at-large member of the New Orleans City Council in 1986 and will author an ordinance aimed at desegregating Mardi Gras. It will prescribe jail time for officers of any club or krewe that uses public resources for its parades and other activities but discriminates on the grounds of "race, gender, handicap or sexual orientation." The ordinance will be introduced in 1991 and passed unanimously in 1992, but not without a great deal of discussion, debate and major outcry from some sections of the white community. Some of her adversaries dub her "The Grinch Who Stole Mardi Gras." Two old-line all-white, all-male Carnival organizations stop parading altogether rather than comply with the non-discrimination ordinance. Over time, however, the organizations integrate peaceably and the number of them increases.

1972 Mahalia Jackson (1911-1972), a best-selling gospel singer whose most popular songs served as metaphors for black strivings for civil and human rights, is given a funeral on February 3 at the Rivergate Convention Center, and buried at Providence Memorial Park in Metairie, just outside the city limits. Born in the Black Pearl section of New Orleans to a longshoreman father and his wife, Jackson began singing in the choir at Mt. Moriah Baptist Church as a young girl before moving to Chicago as a teenager in 1927. After struggling to make a career singing sacred music only, Jackson scored a huge hit in 1948 with a recording of *Move* *on Up a Little Higher* that sold eight million copies. Jackson goes on to become "The Queen of Gospel Music" and, in the words of singer/activist Harry Belafonte, "the single most powerful black woman in the United States." Jackson becomes a close friend of Martin Luther King Jr. and lends her voice to many civil rights gatherings, including the 1963 March on Washington. The internationally acclaimed singer dies in Chicago on January 28, 1972, of a heart attack. Three days later, a first funeral is held in Chicago that attracts a crowd of 60,000. Her New Orleans homegoing ceremony also draws a crowd of thousands and features 24 limousines that drive past her childhood church before moving on to the cemetery.

Thomas Hill (1949-) wins a bronze medal in the 110-meters hurdles in the 1972 Olympics in Munich, Germany. Hill, a graduate of Walter L. Cohen High School, was the world's top-ranked 110-meters hurdler in 1970 as a student at Arkansas State University. After his track career, Hill will earn a doctorate in Counselor Education and work in university administration.

Marcus B. Christian's *Negro Ironworkers of New Orleans: 1718-1900* is published by Pelican Press. It is a ground-breaking study on the contributions of black workers to the building of the city. Christian (1900-1976) was born in what is now part of Houma, LA, and moved to New Orleans in 1917, where he would eventually embark on a career as a writer, editor, poet and historian. The publication of his poem "I am New Orleans" will later lead a local white newspaper columnist to dub him "the Poet Laureate of New Orleans Negroes."

With $2 million ($11.4 million in 2015 dollars) in initial assets, Liberty Bank and Trust Company is founded as an institution with a "sincere interest in community and business development." Norman Francis, president of Xavier University of Louisiana, will serve as the bank's chairman for several years. Alden McDonald Jr., its founding CEO, will guide the bank through more than four decades of growth and expansion and become the dean of African-American bankers in the process. By 2015, Liberty Bank will have branches in eight states (Louisiana, Mississippi, Texas, Illinois, Michigan, Kansas, Missouri and Alabama) and assets of more than $600 million, making it the nation's third largest African-American financial institution. A significant part of Liberty's growth strategy includes acquiring smaller, struggling black banks.

1973 Mark Essex (1949-1973), a Kansas native and former dental technician in the U.S. Navy who received a general discharge on February 10, 1971, for "character and behavior disorders", before making his way to New Orleans, is killed on January 7 after going on a week-long killing spree that begins an hour before midnight--the eleventh hour--on New Year's Eve, December 31, 1972. Essex kills nine people, five of them police officers, and wounds ten others, five of whom also are police officers. Armed with a .44 Magnum carbine rifle, a .38-caliber revolver with the serial number filed off, a gas mask, a couple of strings of firecrackers, a roll of electrical wire, two cans of lighter fluid, a flashlight, a pair of cloth work gloves, and many rounds of ammunition, Essex's escapade ends when he takes refuge on the roof of an 18-story Howard Johnson's hotel in downtown New Orleans and engages in a shootout with police. The siege is aired live on local television and the police use a helicopter to help reach his rooftop position. When Essex exposes himself to shoot at the helicopter, police snipers riddle his body--an autopsy later identifies 200 gunshot wounds. Essex's motives for the killings are alluded to in a handwritten note he sends to a local television station informing them of his impending attack. He said he had many reasons for his actions and that "the death of two innocent brothers will be avenged. And many others." When police later search his apartment, they report that it is covered with "anti-white" graffiti.

1974 Superdome Services, Inc. (SSI) signs a five-year, $8 million ($40.6 million in 2015 dollars) contract with the Louisiana Superdome, then the world's largest indoor sports and entertainment facility, to provide event scheduling, ticket sales, ushering, security, janitorial and landscape maintenance services. SSI is headed by Sherman Copelin, president, and Don Hubbard, assistant project manager, who are also leaders of the Southern Organization for Unified Leadership (SOUL) political organization that helped turn out black voters to elect the state's white governor, Edwin Edwards, in 1972 and the city's white mayor, Maurice "Moon" Landrieu, in 1970 and 1974. When Landrieu persuades the Superdome Commission to award the facility-management contract to SSI, it is considered a political payback and opponents begin mounting objections to SSI's leaders and the firm's performance. In late 1977, SSI's contract will be cancelled. By then, the firm will have grown to employ roughly 3,000 people, many of them black. No other black-owned business will ever perform such a significant role at the Superdome.

The first Bayou Classic football game, pitting Grambling State University against Southern University in New Orleans, takes place on November 23 at Tulane Stadium. Grambling wins 21-0. The series, the nation's largest black college football event, will move in subsequent years to the Mercedes-Benz Superdome. The nationally-televised games, held on the Saturday after Thanksgiving, attract crowds of 50,000-70,000 spectators. However, the games are only the centerpiece of a weekend full of activities that produce an estimated $75 million in tourism revenue for New Orleans as well as funds for the schools.

1975 Paul S. Morton (1950-), a native of Windsor, Ontario, Canada, is installed as senior pastor of Greater St. Stephens Missionary Baptist Church, founded in 1937. An award-winning recording artist as well as a preacher, Morton will lead Greater St. Stephens through a period of tremendous growth--from 647

members to over 20,000--through 2005, when
Hurricane Katrina will devastate the city and its
institutions. In 1992, Morton will co-found the Full
Gospel Baptist Church Fellowship, renaming Greater
St. Stephens as such and making himself a bishop.
Greater St. Stephens will be in the forefront of the
national prosperity-driven, megachurch movement.

Harold Doley Jr. (1947-) founds Doley Securities,
LLC, the oldest investment banking firm in the
United States owned by African Americans. Doley
Securities participates in tens of billions of dollars
in transactions annually involving federal agencies,
state and local governments, international entities,
and corporate and institutional clients. In 1983, Doley
will become the first black person to buy a seat on the
New York Stock Exchange, five years after beginning
his career in investment banking. In 1983, Doley will
also be named an ambassador while serving as U.S.
representative to the African Development Bank and
Fund.

1976 Terrence Duvernay (1943-2001) is appointed chief
administrative officer (CAO) of the City of New
Orleans, making him the first black in the Deep
South to hold such a position of power in a major
city. The appointment is made on May 4 near the
end of Mayor Moon Landrieu's second term in office.
Duvernay will continue his career in the public sector
after his tenure as CAO, serving as deputy director
of the federal Department of Housing and Urban
Development before landing in the private sector as a

vice president of housing and finance at Legg Mason Wood Walker.

....

1977 On November 12, Ernest Nathan "Dutch" Morial (1929-1989) is elected the first black mayor of New Orleans. He will serve two terms in office from 1978-1986. Morial had achieved several other "firsts" before being elected mayor. He had been the first black graduate of Louisiana State University Law School in 1954, the first black member of the Louisiana legislature since the Reconstruction era (1865-1877) in 1967, the first black juvenile court judge in 1970, and the first black judge on the Louisiana Fourth Circuit Court of Appeal in 1974. One of the first major challenges to his administration is a strike by members of the police department in time for Mardi Gras 1979. Parades are cancelled that year but the police union, reputed to be Mafia-controlled, wins no concessions and officers return to work in March.

The Dirty Dozen Brass Band forms and quickly revolutionizes New Orleans brass band music by incorporating funk and bebop into their repertoire, which effectively snatches the brass band sound from the clutches of corny Dixieland and reconnects it to contemporary black culture and the broad reach of soul music. Initially calling themselves the Original Sixth Ward Dirty Dozen, the band was spawned five years earlier by the efforts of banjoist/songwriter/raconteur Danny Barker (1909-1994) to provide training in New Orleans traditional jazz to a group of youth at the Fairview Baptist Church. After landing a few gigs, the Dozen will modify its name and be led by trumpeter Gregory Davis. The energizing danceability of its music will lead new generations of young New Orleans musicians to shamelessly imitate the Dirty Dozen sound with varying degrees of success. The important thing is that the collective efforts of all these brass bands help to make them relevant again in New Orleans culture in the streets, the clubs, on the concert stage and on the radio.

1978 In front of a crowd of 65,000 at the Louisiana Superdome, Muhammad Ali wins a unanimous 15-round decision over Leon Spinks to win the world heavyweight boxing title for an unprecedented third time. Ali had previously lost his title to Spinks in February 1978 in a match in Las Vegas. This rematch in New Orleans will be Ali's last victory as a professional boxer.

1980 The total population of New Orleans is 557,482, according to the census: 308,136 Negro (55.3%), 236,967 White (42.5%) and 12,379 Other (2.2%). Black people constitute a majority of the population for the first time since the 1830 census. The influx of refugees from Vietnam and other parts of Southeast Asia at the conclusion of the Vietnam War accounts for the significant increase in the Other population category.

Interurban Broadcasting Group, headed by Chicagoans Tom Lewis (1936-2011) and Jim Hutchinson (1947-), purchases WYLD AM and FM stations, providing black ownership for the first time to New Orleans radio. WYLD-FM's urban contemporary format will make it the top-rated station in the market throughout the mid-1980s. Interurban Broadcasting Group will file for bankruptcy protection several years later and will sell WYLD, which will become white-owned and in the fold of Clear Channel Communications. WBOK and WYLD (then operating as WMRY), beginning in 1949 and 1950, respectively, were the first integrated radio stations in New Orleans and made a place for pioneering black broadcast personalities such as George "Tex" Stephens, Dr. Daddy-O (Vernon Winslow), Ernie the Whip, James "Okey-Dokey" Smith, Shelley Pope, Groovy Gus and Larry McKinley.

Gordon Plaza subdivision is developed featuring 67 new modern single-family homes developed principally for black buyers by a black contractor. Unfortunately, no one tells the home buyers that their homes sit on the site of the former Agriculture Street Landfill, closed in 1958. The area later tests positive for several hazardous, carcinogenic elements and compounds. In 1994, the site is placed on the Environmental Protection Agency's priority list for remediation. Suits by residents will drag through the courts for decades. Also built on the same landfill site are 262 units of public housing, Press Park, and a public school, Moton Elementary, that will eventually be abandoned.

The second fight between boxers "Sugar" Ray Leonard and Roberto Duran takes place in the Louisiana

Superdome on November 25. Leonard, who lost the first bout, wins by technical knockout in the eighth round when Duran says "No mas" and stops fighting. The fight, which is one of the most famous events in boxing history, was promoted by Don King. It draws a live audience of 25,038 and generates $38 ($116.3 million in 2015 dollars) million in total revenue from closed circuit and delayed broadcasts as well as ticket sales.

1983 Dillard University sells its Flint-Goodridge Hospital to a national medical chain for $1.8 million ($4.3 million in 2015 dollars). At the time of the sale, the facility is a 128-bed hospital but university officials claim it costs the school $2 million ($4.8 million in 2015 dollars) a year to operate. An effort by local black doctors to buy the hospital fails.

1984 Echelon Construction Co., owned by Anthony "Chuck" Mercadel (1937-2002), co-builds the Louisiana Pavilion and serves as sole contractor of the Aquacade for the 1984 Louisiana Exposition, which is held May 12-November 11. Mercadel, the first state-licensed African-American construction superintendent in Louisiana, also partners in the construction of the Fulton Street Mall, the Italian Plaza and the Spanish Plaza renovation for the world's fair. The other noteworthy involvement of black folks in the world's fair is the Afro-American Pavilion, "I've Known Rivers," a $3.2 million ($7.4 million in 2015 dollars) attraction spearheaded by civic leader Sybil Morial and artist John T. Scott. The pavilion serves as a prototype for other black history and culture museums around the United States.

1985 On January 20, Warren Woodfork is appointed Superintendent of the New Orleans Police Department, the first black person to hold this position since the founding of the police department in 1796. By the 1990s, the NOPD ranks will be half-black.

Everett Williams, Ph.D. (1930-2013) is appointed the first black superintendent of New Orleans public schools. He will serve in this capacity until 1992. A native New Orleanian, Williams earned his bachelor's and master's degrees at Xavier University of Louisiana and his doctorate at Michigan State. He began teaching in New Orleans public schools in 1957.

1986 Sidney John Barthelemy (1942-) is sworn into office on May 5 as the second black mayor of New Orleans. He will serve two terms from 1986-1994.

The City of New Orleans pays more than $2.8 million ($6 million in 2015 dollars) to settle lawsuits alleging police brutality. The suits were filed by 13 black residents of the Algiers section of the city, stemming from an incident several years earlier. In November 1980, after a white police officer, Gregory Neupert, was found shot to death in his patrol car near a public housing project in that neighborhood, fellow officers went on a rampage in the quest to find his killer. In the process, they shot and killed Raymond Ferdinand, 38, an alleged informant, after claiming he lunged at officers with a pocket knife. The cops tortured several other people and claimed to have forced a confession out of an informant regarding the identity of the killers. They then stormed the homes of the two suspects simultaneously, killing James Billy, 26, at one location and Reginald Miles, 28, and his girlfriend, Sherry Singleton, 26, at another. When one of the black officers on the raid, Oris Buckner, refuted the official explanation that Billy, Miles and Singleton fired shots at officers before being gunned down, a state grand jury declined to indict any of the seven white officers involved in the executions. However, a federal grand jury indicted them on conspiracy to violate civil rights. Three of the seven policemen were convicted in 1983 and sent to prison; the other four were acquitted. Buckner received immunity for his testimony. The suit settled by the City names 55 officers for acts of brutality.

1987 Chef Louis Evans (1940 or 1941-1990) becomes only the second Louisianian to be elected to membership in the Order of the Golden Toque, a 100-member national organization of chefs. Evans works mainly at high-end white-owned restaurants, beginning in 1959 as a cook at Sclafani's in Metairie. Ten years later, he joined the staff of the Pontchartrain Hotel's highly acclaimed Caribbean Room. Promoted to executive chef in 1973, he spends 18 years at the Pontchartrain before moving to Kabby's at the Hilton in 1987.

1990 The total population of New Orleans is 496,938, according to the census: 307,728 Black (62%),

173,554 White (35%), 759 American Indian (.1%), 9,678 Asian (1.9%), 5,219 Other Race (1%).

1991 On January 3, William Jennings Jefferson (1947-) begins the first of nine two-year terms as a member of the United States House of Representatives for Louisiana's Second District, which encompasses New Orleans. Jefferson will be Louisiana's first black congressman since the Reconstruction era (1865-1877). He will lose an election for a tenth term in office on December 6, 2008, in an upset to Joseph Cao, a Republican of Vietnamese descent, in the midst of a bribery investigation that will eventually send Jefferson to prison.

1992 Revius Ortique Jr. (1924-2008) is the first black person elected to the Louisiana Supreme Court. The former civil rights attorney and activist will serve on the court until his 70th birthday in June 1994, the court's mandatory age for retirement.

John T. Scott (1940-2007), sculptor, painter, printmaker, collagist, receives the MacArthur Fellowship, the "genius award." Scott had taught art at his alma mater, Xavier University of Louisiana, since 1965.

A U.S. Department of Justice study reports that residents of New Orleans filed more complaints about police brutality to the federal government between 1984 and 1990 than any other city in the nation. The majority of the complaints came from Afro-Orleanians.

1993 New Orleans leads the nation in homicides with a rate of 80 per 100,000. The victims and their killers are mostly young, poor, male and black. By 2013, the rate will have been cut in half to 41 per 100,000 and the city will be ranked fifth in the nation among cities with populations of at least 50,000 people.

Warren McDaniels (1944-2008) is the first black appointed to be superintendent of the New Orleans Fire Department (NOFD). A high school dropout who later earned his GED and an associate's degree in fire prevention, McDaniels joined the NOFD in 1969 and worked his way up the ranks. He will serve as fire chief until retiring in 2002.

1994 The U.S. Park Service creates the New Orleans Jazz National Historical Park to explain and celebrate the city's role as the birthplace of jazz, America's greatest contribution to world culture, which was created, molded and refined largely by black men.

Marc Haydel Morial (1958-) is sworn in as the third black mayor of New Orleans on May 2. The son of the city's first black mayor, Dutch Morial, the younger Morial will serve two terms from 1994-2002.

Marshall Faulk (1973-), a New Orleans native who attended Carver High School before embarking on an outstanding college football career as a three-time All-America running back at San Diego State University, signs a seven-year $17.2 million contract on July 25 to play for the Indianapolis Colts of the

National Football League (NFL) and receives a $5.1 million signing bonus. At the time, this is the largest professional contract awarded to any New Orleans professional athlete. Faulk will become the first NFL player to win both the Offensive Rookie of the Year Award and the Pro Bowl's Most Valuable Player Award in the same season. He also will be the first rookie to win Pro Bowl MVP. Faulk will later be named All-Pro three times before finishing his professional football career in 2006, becoming a sports commentator on television and getting elected to the NFL Hall of Fame in 2011.

After recording 421 homicides for the year, New Orleans earns the distinction of being the Murder Capital of America for a second year in a row with a per capita homicide rate of 85.8 per 100,000 residents. It's a title the city will win again in later years, despite experiencing a low of 199 murders in 1999.

1995 The Essence Music Festival is held in New Orleans to celebrate the 25th anniversary of the founding of *Essence* Magazine, headquartered in New York City. Dubbed "the party with a purpose," the event will go on to become an annual gathering held on the Fourth of July weekend, principally in the Mercedes-Benz Superdome and the Ernest Morial New Orleans Convention Center. Attracting crowds in excess of 400,000, the Essence Festival will soon become one of the largest celebrations of African-American music and culture in the world.

On October 20, New Orleans Police Officer Antoinette Frank (1971-) is sentenced to death for the killing of fellow black officer Ronald Williams and two Vietnamese workers at the Kim Anh Restaurant on March 4, 1995. Frank and her lover/accomplice Rogers Lacaze had botched a robbery of the restaurant shortly after closing hours. Frank had worked off-duty details at the restaurant and knew where the owners usually kept their cash. After her third visit to the eatery that evening, suspicious owner Chau Vu moved the cash to another location and hid in the restaurant's freezer as the robbery commenced. Unable to locate the cash, Frank and Lacaze shoot and kill Williams and two members of the clean-up crew who cannot tell them where to find the owner or the cash. Upon conviction and sentencing, Frank becomes the first NOPD officer to be sentenced to death--and the second woman on death row in Louisiana in the 1990s.

1996 Len Davis (1954-), a decorated New Orleans police officer who ran a drug-protection racket, is sentenced to death on April 26 for a hit he ordered on Kim Groves, a 32-year-old African-American mother of three and security guard who had reported Davis and his partner for police brutality against one of her neighbors in 1994. Davis, the only police officer to have received a federal death sentence, was overheard on an FBI wiretap ordering and celebrating the murder. That same FBI wiretap operation resulted in the convictions of six other New Orleans police officers on drug trafficking charges.

1998 Percy Miller (1970-), known professionally as Master P, releases *MP The Last Don* on his own No Limit Records in early June. The seventh album of his career, it debuts at #1 on the Billboard Top 200 charts selling over 400,000 copies in its first week. It will go on to sell over four million copies, making it the best-selling album of Miller's career and one of the seminal works in the gangsta rap genre. It is Miller's business acumen, however, that is even more noteworthy. After returning to his hometown New Orleans in 1995 from his previous base of operations, Richmond, CA, Miller signs a ground-breaking music distribution deal the following year with Priority Records in which No Limit Records will retain 100% ownership of its master recordings and keep 85% of its records' sales while giving Priority 15% in return for pressing and distribution. The deal earns Miller hundreds of millions of dollars, money which he then uses to expand his holdings in areas outside the music industry, including a travel agency; an athletic-shoe retail outlet; real estate; film, music, and television production; toy manufacturing; a phone sex company; clothing; telecommunications; book & magazine publishing; car rims and accessories; fast food franchises; gas stations; and a sports management agency. Miller's empire-building strategies will be been imitated by others around the globe. Despite the failures of some of his enterprises, in 2013 he will be listed as #3 on Forbes Magazine's list of richest moguls in hip-hop, with an estimated worth of $350 million.

2000 The total population of New Orleans is 484,674, according to the census: 325,947 Black or African American (67.3%), 135,956 White (28.1%), 10,972 Asian (2.3%), 991 American Indian (.2%), 10,699 Other Race and Two or More Races (2.2%). This is the largest number of black residents in the history of the city.

2002 Clarence Ray Nagin (1956-) is sworn in as the fourth black mayor of New Orleans on May 6. He will serve two terms from 2002-2010 and will be the last of four consecutive black men elected as mayor. Four years later, Nagin will be convicted of public corruption for deeds he commits while in office.

Eddie Jack Jordan Jr. is elected the first black district attorney for New Orleans on November 5. He will resign his position in late 2007 under pressure from several sections of the white community. On March 30, 2005, Jordan will be found liable for racial discrimination by a federal jury for the mass firing of forty-three white employees immediately after taking office. These employees, who had worked for the previous D.A., a white man who held the office for 30 years, were replaced almost entirely by African Americans. The Orleans Parish District Attorney's Office will be required to pay $2.4 million to the plaintiffs. Jordan will lose an appeal of the case. In late 2006, a grand jury will indict seven New Orleans Police Department officers on first-degree murder charges for the death of two unarmed men, and the attempted cover-up of the crime, on the Danzinger

Bridge in the turmoil after Hurricane Katrina. As a result, Jordan's office will draw the ire and enmity of the NOPD, its union and many of its supporters. Cooperation between the police department and the D.A.'s office will sink to an all-time low, hampering the effectiveness of Jordan's operation. In July 2007, the D.A.'s office will release a suspect in the murders of five teens because it is unable to find a key witness in the case; the NOPD will hold a press conference a short time later at which police officials present the witness. Critics will also complain that the murder and attempted murder conviction rate for Jordan's office is only 12 percent in 2003 and 2004, compared to the 80 percent national average. They will also scoff at the D.A.'s overall prosecution rate of only 7 percent. Increasing numbers of white officials will begin calling for Jordan's resignation; he will finally give in on October 30, 2007.

In March, the Housing Authority of New Orleans is taken over by the U.S. Department of Housing and Urban Development and managed directly by the federal government. This arrangement, which will continue until May 2014, comes on the heels of a cooperative endeavor agreement between the city agency and the federal department that began in 1996. Despite the change in management, living conditions for the virtually all-black residents in the city's public housing developments continue to worsen.

2004 Marlin Gusman, a former New Orleans City Councilperson, is elected Criminal Sheriff of Orleans

Parish on November 2, the first black person to hold this office. In 2010, the Criminal and Civil Sheriff offices will be combined in Orleans Parish and Gusman will be elected to the consolidated position as Sheriff of Orleans Parish. Gusman's office has oversight of Orleans Parish Prison, one of the most notorious jails in the nation.

2005 Brenda Marie Osbey (1957-) is named Poet Laureate of Louisiana by Governor Kathleen Blanco on the recommendation of a panel of peers from the arts and humanities. She is the first Louisiana poet laureate to be selected through a merit-driven process. Osbey's first collection, *Ceremony for Minneconjoux* (Callalloo Press), was published in 1983. Her fourth book, *All Saints: New and Selected Poems* (LSU Press), won the American Book Award in 1997. Osbey spends most of her two-year tenure as Louisiana Poet Laureate traveling the country discussing the state of New Orleans in the aftermath of Hurricane Katrina and the failure of the city's levee system.

Restaurateur Willie Mae Seaton (1916-2015), proprietor of Willie Mae's Scotch House, which is famous for its fried chicken, receives the American Classic Award from the James Beard Foundation, the leading national organization promoting the culinary arts.

On June 27, cultural icon Allison "Tootie" Montana (1922-2005) collapses and dies while speaking in New Orleans City Council chambers against police harassment of Mardi Gras/Black Indians. Montana had been acknowledged as the Chief of Chiefs of the gangs of Afro-Orleanians who mask as Native Americans in elaborate, colorful, self-made costumes during Mardi Gras and at other select times of the year. Montana had been named a National Endowment for the Arts Heritage Fellow in 1987 in recognition of his outstanding contributions to the Mardi Gras/ Black Indian culture as long-time chief of the Yellow Pocahontas tribe, his innovative costumes (called suits), and his enthusiastic singing and dancing. He had masked for 52 years before his death.

Hurricane Katrina makes landfall on August 29 as a Category 3 storm with winds in excess of 125 miles per hour a few miles south and east of New Orleans. It will become "the single most catastrophic natural disaster in U.S. history," according to the federal government, causing over $108 billion in damage to New Orleans and other places on the Gulf Coast. The federal levee system designed to protect the city from storm water breaches in 51 places. Roughly 80% of New Orleans floods, including more than 107,000 properties. In some places the waters are 10-15 feet high. Altogether, roughly 39% or 182,000 properties suffer damage related to the storm. More than 1,500 people in Louisiana die. Despite orders to evacuate the city prior to the storm, many residents stay in their homes and are stranded during the subsequent flooding. They later have to be rescued by boat and helicopter. Thousands of others seek refuge on highway overpasses, at the Louisiana Superdome and at the city's convention center. New Orleans then has to be forcibly evacuated for six weeks and house-to-house searches conducted. Over the next few months, 7,500 mostly-black public school system employees are summarily fired as are thousands more government workers, including staffers at City Hall and Charity Hospital. Ten years later, more than 100,000 former black residents will continue to be exiled; all the major public housing complexes will be torn down and rebuilt as mixed-income developments operated by non-governmental entities providing far fewer units of subsidized housing; the New Orleans public school system will be converted into a network of charter schools with non-union educators and a teacher corps that is only half black, down from 71% before the storm. In the meantime, achievement test scores, graduation rates and other measures of success will reportedly improve significantly for black students in the city's public schools over the next ten years, though there will be significant questions raised about how those figures are arrived at. Nevertheless, the net effect of these disaster-enabled changes results in disempowerment and dispossession of New Orleans by black people in areas such as public education, public housing, public health care, government, and policies for awarding rebuilding grants to homeowners.

2007 WBOK-AM returns to the airwaves on November 3 with new owner Bakewell Media of Louisiana, LLC, headed by New Orleans native Danny Bakewell Sr. It becomes the first black-owned radio station with an all-talk format and provides a forum for Afro-Orleanians and others to discuss, analyze and opine about the state of New Orleans and the world from a black perspective. The devastation wrought on the city's black community during and after Hurricane Katrina will be the chief topic of discussion for several years.

Irma Thomas (1941-), arguably the greatest R&B singer to come out of the New Orleans music scene, wins a Grammy Award in the Contemporary Blues Album category for *After the Rain.* Thomas, born in Ponchatoula, LA, and brought to live in New Orleans at an early age, had scored her first hit in 1960 when the single *(You Can Have My Husband but) Don't Mess with My Man* reached #22 on the Billboard R&B chart. That was followed by a string of other New Orleans soul classics released in the 1960s, songs like *It's Raining, Ruler of My Heart, I Done Got Over, Time is on My Side, Wish Someone Would Care*, and *Breakaway.* Thomas will also go on to become a perennially popular live performer, an embodiment of New Orleans Soul.

2009 Avery "Little General" Johnson (1965-), who led St. Augustine High School to a 35-0 record and a state championship in 1983, hits the championship-winning shot for the San Antonio Spurs in game five of the National Basketball Association finals against the New York Knicks, making him the first New Orleanian to be an NBA champion. Johnson, who played point guard for the Spurs and five other teams over the course of his 16-year professional career, will go on to become a coach in the NBA and an analyst for television after his playing days end.

....

2010 The total population of New Orleans is 343,829, according to the census: 206,871 Black or African American (60.2%), 113,428 White (33%), 1,047 American Indian (.3%), 9,970 Asian (2.9%), 12,379 Other Race and Two or More Races (3.6%). Overall, there are 140,845 fewer residents than in 2000; the black population officially declines by 119,076 over the same period.

Mitchell Landrieu (1960-) is sworn in as mayor on May 3, making him the first white person to hold the office since his father, Moon, finished a second term in 1978. Landrieu is elected in a landslide, garnering 66% of the vote in an open primary. Black voters are nearly 60% of the electorate at the time and vote for him in overwhelming numbers despite the presence of other black candidates in the race. It was Landrieu's third try for the office; he ran unsuccessfully in 1994 and 2006.

Susan Hutson (1968?-), a black attorney who had been serving as the assistant inspector general for the City of Los Angeles, is hired as the first independent police monitor for New Orleans. Her role is to review civilian and internal complaints about the New Orleans Police Department in addition to analyzing internal police investigations, disciplinary actions, police shootings, reports of use of force and in-custody deaths.

2011 The National Endowment for the Arts bestows the Jazz Masters Award on the Marsalis Family--patriarch Ellis (1934-) and sons Branford (1960-), Wynton (1961-), Delfeayo (1965-) and Jason (1977-). It is the first time the award is made to a group, not a single person, though the music culture in New Orleans is often transmitted through families.

Theodore "Bo" Dollis (1944-2015), big chief of the Wild Magnolias Mardi Gras/Black Indian gang, receives the National Heritage Fellowship from the National Endowment for the Arts. In 1970, Dollis sang the lead on a recording, *Handa Wanda*, which mixed Mardi Gras/Black Indian chants with funk instrumentation. In 1974, an entire genre-creating album called *The Wild Magnolias* was released with such noted New Orleans musicians as Earl Turbinton, Willie Tee and Uganda Roberts backing Dollis.

New Orleans once again claims the dubious distinction of Murder Capital of America with a per capita murder rate of 57.6/per 100,000. The city has been a perennial top-five murder leader for decades but violent crime rates dropped for a few years after Hurricane Katrina in late 2005. Additionally, the city's 2011 incarceration rate remains the highest in the world at 912 per 100,000, much lower than the 2000 peak of 1,298 per 100,000, but still 3.8 times higher than the national average of 236 per 100,000. These statistics continue to earn the city right to be called the "Crime and Punishment Capital of America."

"The New Orleans Police Department has long been a troubled agency," a report from the Civil Rights Division of the U.S. Department of Justice declares. "Basic elements of effective policing--clear policies, training, accountability and confidence of the citizenry--have been absent for years. Far too often, officers show a lack of respect for the civil rights and dignity of the people of New Orleans...too many officers of every rank either do not understand or choose to ignore the boundaries of constitutional policing." Two years later the police department will enter into a consent decree under which it is monitored by a federal judge.

New Orleans finally relinquishes its dubious distinction as the most blighted city in America when it registers a 21% rate for abandoned houses. That level is bested by Detroit and Flint, Michigan, at 23% and 24%, respectively. New Orleans has recorded one of the highest rates of blighted property since 1994.

2012 Fred Luter Jr. (1956-), New Orleans native and senior pastor of Franklin Avenue Baptist Church, is elected the first black president of the Southern Baptist Convention on June 19. Founded in 1845, the Southern Baptist Convention claims a membership of 16 million individuals and 45,000 churches.

Prolific songwriter/arranger/producer/performer Allen Toussaint (1938-2015) receives the National Medal of Arts from President Barack Obama. His music helped define New Orleans rhythm and blues in the 1960s and '70s and provided hits for many other artists--Ernie K-Doe, Irma Thomas, Lee Dorsey, Benny Spellman, LaBelle, the Pointer Sisters, the Rolling Stones and several others. Toussaint will die of a heart attack after a performance in Madrid, Spain, on November 9, 2015.

In May, former nine-term Congressman William J. Jefferson begins serving a 13-year sentence in a federal penitentiary for a 2009 conviction on bribery. It is the longest sentence ever received by a member of Congress. During this period, several of Jefferson's siblings will also be convicted or plead guilty to other felonies related to their abuse of the family's political power. In addition to the Jeffersons, several other minor public officials, civil servants and politically-connected business people of this era will be convicted of such crimes as accepting bribes, defrauding insurance companies and the federal government, embezzlement and other larcenous activities.

Winston Burns Sr. (1925-), younger brother of civil rights activist Leonard Burns, is awarded the Congressional Gold Medal for his service as a U.S. Marine in World War II. Receiving the prestigious recognition more than 60 years after his last active duty assignment, Burns was one of 20,000 black men known as the Montford Point Marines. The moniker came from the name of the segregated boot camp in North Carolina where black recruits were trained from 1942-1949, even though the Marines were ordered to integrate their ranks in 1941. Burns enlisted in

January 1943 and continued to serve until 1951. He later had a successful career as a teacher and coach in New Orleans public schools.

In December, Sheriff Marlin Gusman signs a consent decree with the U.S. Department of Justice that mandates increased staffing and training for deputies at the Orleans Parish Prison, which has been riddled with problems related to inmate deaths and violence, frequent escapes, poor mental health care and smuggling in of drugs, alcohol, weapons, phones and other contraband.

2013 Bernette Joshua Johnson (1945-) is sworn in as the first black Chief Justice of the Louisiana Supreme Court, which was established in 1813. Elected to the court from the Seventh Supreme Court District of Louisiana, which encompasses New Orleans, Johnson is the second African-American on the court (after Revius Ortique) and its first black female justice. Johnson, who has served on the court since 1994, merits the Chief Justice role due to her seniority on the court when her predecessor, Catherine Kimball, retires. Johnson is the court's 25th Chief Justice.

Kenneth Polite, a 37-year-old New Orleans native with degrees from Harvard and Georgetown Law School, begins his tenure as the Eastern District of Louisiana's U.S. attorney on September 20. Polite is the area's first black U.S. attorney. His appointment to the post comes after the resignation of his predecessor due to misconduct by prosecutors in the U.S. attorney's office.

According to data for this year collected by the U.S. Census Bureau, income inequality is far greater in New Orleans 295 years after its founding than it is in the rest of the country. The ratio of the income of the top 5 percent of households to the bottom 20 percent is 15 to 1 in New Orleans, compared to 9 to 1 nationally. The top 5 percent in New Orleans earn at least $189,737 annually, while the bottom 20 percent earn less than $12,301. The national threshold for the bottom 20 percent is an annual salary of $21,433. In 2013, the annual median household income for black families in New Orleans is $27,812--54 percent lower than white families in the metro region and 20 percent lower than black households nationally. Thirty percent of white households in New Orleans earn more than $105,910, compared with 7 percent of African-Americans; 44 percent of black households earn less than $20,900, compared with 17 percent of white households. The poverty rate in New Orleans in 2013 is 27 percent; the national rate is 14.5. After centuries of struggling for economic equality, this is where we ended up: 15 to 1 and 54%.

2014 On February 12, Clarence Ray Nagin, the fourth black mayor of New Orleans (2002-2010) and the 60th in the history of the city, becomes the first former New Orleans mayor to be convicted of a felony when he is found guilty on 20 charges of public corruption (bribery, wire fraud, tax evasion, conspiracy). He is later ordered to forfeit $501,200 that prosecutors calculated as funds he received in the bribery schemes for which he was convicted. The sum included travel paid by city vendors, cellular telephone service, and money meant to appear as investments in Stone Age, a granite company owned by his sons. The forfeiture amount also includes ill-gotten business for Stone Age and the monetary value of free granite provided to the company by people doing business with the city. On July 9, Nagin is sentenced to 10 years in a federal penitentiary and ordered to pay $82,000 in restitution. Interestingly enough, Nagin, a cable community executive who had never held public office, was elected in 2002 as an anti-corruption "business candidate," receiving a majority of the white vote and a minority of the black vote. But in 2006, when he runs for a second term, he is elected with a majority of the black vote and a minority of the white vote. This twist occurs because when the failure of the federally-built levees lead to the flooding and evacuation of New Orleans, Nagin resists attempts by power brokers in the white community to keep the largely black sections of the city from being redeveloped. When he declares at a 2006 MLK Day Rally that New Orleans will be a "Chocolate City" again despite what the folks "Uptown" wanted, he is vilified in many parts of the white community, including its media. When the white power structure's hand-picked candidate, then Lt. Governor Mitchell Landrieu, loses to Nagin in the 2006 mayoral race, Nagin's enemies seek other means to defeat him. In the end, and with Nagin's complicity, they succeed.

Reginald Adams, 61, is released from prison on May 12 after serving 34 years on the false accusation of murdering a white policeman's wife in 1979. The victim had been shot seven times in her home and some of her jewelry was found to be missing. New Orleans Police Department detectives and then-District Attorney Harry Connick Sr.'s office received evidence that the murder weapon in the case was traced to two other suspects but they never turned that evidence over to Adams' attorney. Adams claimed the police secured his confession after questioning him for four hours and forcing him to drink alcohol and take Valium, a muscle relaxer. The person he initially confessed to murdering was a dark-haired male, not a blond woman. Nevertheless, Adams will be convicted twice in jury trials of killing the white woman. Years later, the policeman whose wife was the murder victim is convicted of murdering his second wife and one of the assistant district attorneys who prosecuted the Adams case became a judge and was convicted of corruption. The Adams case was not the only one in which prosecutors and New Orleans police deliberately withheld evidence that would have freed black citizens. By the time of the Adams ruling, nine of the 36 people sent to death row by D.A. Connick's prosecutors have had their convictions overturned because of misconduct on the part of the prosecution.

In May, New Orleans native Dean Baquet (1956-) is named executive editor of The New York Times. Baquet began his career in the 1970s as a reporter for the New Orleans States-Item and the Times-Picayune before winning a Pulitzer Prize at the Chicago Tribune for a series on governmental corruption. He later served as managing editor of the Los Angeles Times before landing the top spot at the New York Times.

Rudy Lombard, Ph.D. (1939-2014), the lead plaintiff in the famous 1963 *Lombard v Louisiana* decision by the U.S. Supreme Court which paved the way for the desegregation of public accommodations in the country, dies of cancer on December 13. Lombard, who had been president of the local chapter of the activist Congress of Racial Equality (CORE) at the time of that initial arrest, would go on to become vice-chairman of the CORE national board of directors and train hundreds of Freedom Riders. After earning a Ph.D. in Urban Studies in 1970 from Syracuse University, Lombard co-founded the New Orleans Neighborhood Development Foundation, a first-time homebuyers training program for low-income people. He also spearheaded the Claiborne Avenue Design Team, which produced a visionary plan in 1976 for overcoming the physical, economic and cultural disruption of an eight-mile stretch of Claiborne Avenue in the downtown section of the city that had been created by the building of an overpass through there as part of the federal Interstate 10 highway. Later, Lombard would also go on to produce *The New Orleans Creole Feast* in 1978, a cookbook (and later an accompanying food festival) featuring 319 recipes by 15 important but little-heralded black master chefs who created several of the iconic dishes associated with the world renowned cuisine of New Orleans.

2015 An amendment to the Home Rule Charter of New
Orleans requiring the City to establish and maintain a
Disadvantaged Business Enterprise (DBE) program to
award City contracts to businesses owned by people
of color and women goes into effect on January 1.
Approved by voters in an election on November 4,
2014, the charter change also removes the mayor
from the selection process for major city contracts
and instead gives the responsibility to selection
committees comprised of experts in the fields for
which the contracts are awarded. The change has
been supported by government-reform groups
and is expected to provide meaningful economic
opportunities to black-owned businesses. For 2014,
the administration of Mayor Mitchell Landrieu reports
that "certified DBE firms were awarded approximately
$21.3 million in new business opportunities with the
City of New Orleans, representing 37% of the total value
of contracts awarded this year." The administration's
target had been to award 35% of contract values to
DBEs.

Fernand Cheri III (1952-) is ordained as auxiliary
bishop of the Archdiocese of New Orleans on March
23. Cheri is the first black New Orleans native to
hold the post and only the fourth black to serve as
the city's auxiliary bishop for the Catholic Church.
Bishop Harold Perry, the first black auxiliary bishop,
had been appointed 50 years earlier in 1965.

On June 30, Norman C. Francis (1931-) officially
retires as president of Xavier University of Louisiana

(XULA) after 47 years as head of the institution. He steps down with the additional distinction of being the longest-tenured leader of an American university. During Francis' leadership of Xavier, the Catholic university grew to become the leading producer of blacks earning bachelor's degrees in biology, chemistry, physics, and physical sciences and the leading producer of black students who later go on to earn medical degrees. Francis's record as a builder includes tripling the school's enrollment to over 3,500 students, expanding the campus from 5 buildings contained in a city block to 16 structures on over 63 acres of land, and growing the university's endowment from under $20 million to over $160 million. Francis, born in Lafayette, LA, was an alumnus of Xavier who later earned a law degree at Loyola University of New Orleans (1955, a black first) and then went on to serve a stint in the U.S. Army (1956-57) before coming back to the school as an administrator and eventually being selected in 1968 as the first lay leader of the religious institution. C. Reynold Verret, a native of Haiti and an experienced university administrator with a Ph.D. in Biochemistry from the Massachusetts Institute of Technology, is named to succeed Francis.

David Francis (1959-), son of Norman Francis, is named publisher of the 178-year-old *Times-Picayune* newspaper and its online counterpart, NOLA. com. The announcement is made in mid-June. Francis, who earned an MBA at Tulane University, becomes the first African-American publisher of the media property. He was the business manager for before being named associate publisher in 2013, another historic achievement. Like many American print media companies, the *Times-Picayune* has experienced several years of declining revenues, readership and personnel in the transition from paper to online delivery systems before turning to Francis for leadership.

The average daily number of incarcerated people in Orleans Parish Prison is roughly 1,900 as of April 2015, a two-thirds decrease from June 30, 2005, when the average daily rate was 5,919. Equally revealing, the city's crime rate shows a decrease corresponding to the lower incarceration rate. Unfortunately, 85% of all the people incarcerated at the prison are black.

The husband and wife photographer team Keith Calhoun and Chandra McCormick are the first New Orleans artists to be selected to exhibit their work at the Venice Biennale, the world's most prestigious visual arts exhibition. Calhoun and McCormick exhibit their documentary photographs of neo-slavery at the maximum-security Louisiana State Penitentiary, an 18,000-acre, 6,000-inmate former plantation commonly known as Angola and The Farm.

TO BE CONTINUED...

Selected Bibliography

The genesis of this project lies in a timeline the poet and essayist Brenda Marie Osbey created in the late 1970s based on her research into French and Spanish colonial archival documents. Some of this material made its way into her multi-part series of articles, "Faubourg Tremé: A Community in Transition," published in the late 1980s and later into her course "Black New Orleans," which she has taught at several universities around the United States since the early 1990s.

I have added to this seminal effort, expanded the chronology into the 21st century and filled in some mini-narratives that convey, I hope, the richness of the black presence in this distinctive city.

There is now more information than ever available to researchers in books and articles, on the Internet and in archives. I have drawn on many of these sources to flesh out this chronology and to craft this Afro-centered perspective. However, in order to adhere to my intention to make this compilation an example of popular history and analysis--and not an academic treatise--I will only list a few key materials that can serve as gateways to those interested in further research.

SECONDARY SOURCES

BOOKS

Arnesen, Eric. *Waterfront Workers of New Orleans: Race, Class and Politics, 1863-1923.* New York: Oxford University Press, 1991.

Bell, Caryn Cossé. *Revolution, Romanticism, and the Afro-Creole Protest Tradition in Louisiana 1718-1868.* Baton Rouge: Louisiana State University Press, 1997.

Blassingame, John W. *Black New Orleans 1860-1880.* Chicago: University of Chicago Press, 1973.

Boelhower, William, editor. *New Orleans in the Atlantic World: Between Land and Sea.* New York: Routledge, 2010.

Buerkle, Jack V. and Danny Barker. *Bourbon Street Black: The New Orleans Black Jazzman.* New York: Oxford University Press, 1975.

Campanella, Richard. *Bienville's Dilemma: A Historical Geography of New Orleans.* Lafayette, LA: Center for Louisiana Studies, University of Louisiana at Lafayette, 2008.

Desdunes, Rodolphe Lucien. *Our People and Our History*, Translated and Edited by Sister Dorothea Olga McCants. Baton Rouge: Louisiana State University Press, 1973.

Dessens, Nathalie. *From Saint-Domingue to New Orleans: Migration and Influences.* Gainesville: University Press of Florida, 2007.

Evans, Freddi Williams. *Congo Square: African Roots in New Orleans.* Lafayette, LA: University of Louisiana at Lafayette Press, 2011.

MacDonald, Robert R., John Randolph Kemp and Edward F. Haas, general editors. *Louisiana's Black Heritage.* New Orleans: Louisiana State Museum, 1979.

Christian, Marcus. *Negro Iron Workers in Louisiana 1718-1900.* Gretna, LA: Pelican Publishing Company, 1972.

_____. *A Black History of Louisiana.* Unpublished, University of New Orleans Library, 1980.

Dawdy, Shannon Lee. *Building the Devil's Empire: French Colonial New Orleans.* Chicago: The University of Chicago Press, 2008.

DeVore, Donald E. *Defying Jim Crow: African American Community Development and the Struggle for Racial Equality in New Orleans, 1900-1960.* Baton Rouge: Louisiana State University Press, 2015.

Fairclough, Adam. *Race & Democracy: The Civil Rights Struggle in Louisiana, 1915-1972.* Athens, GA: University of Georgia Press, 1995.

Flucker, Turry and Phoenix Savage. *Images of America: African Americans of New Orleans*. Charleston, SC: Arcadia Publishing, 2010.

Hall, Gwendolyn Midlo. *Africans in Colonial Louisiana: The Development of Afro-Creole Culture in the Eighteenth Century*. Baton Rouge: Louisiana State University Press, 1992.

Hair, William Ivy. *Carnival of Fury: Robert Charles and the New Orleans Race Riot of 1900*. Baton Rouge: Louisiana State University Press, 1976.

Hanger, Kimberly A. *Bounded Lives, Bounded Places: Free Black Society in Colonial New Orleans, 1769–1803*. Durham, NC: Duke University Press, 1997.

Hirsch, Arnold R. and Joseph Logsdon, editors. *Creole New Orleans: Race and Americanization*. Baton Rouge: Louisiana State University Press, 1992.

Ingersoll, Thomas N. *Mammon and Manon in Early New Orleans*. Knoxville, TN: University of Tennessee Press, 1999.

Johnson, Walter. *Soul by Soul: Life inside the Antebellum Slave Mart*. Cambridge, MA: Harvard University Press, 1999.

Kein, Sybil, editor. *Creole: The History and Legacy of Louisiana's Free People of Color*, Baton Rouge: Louisiana State University Press, 2000.

Kmen, Henry A. *Music in New Orleans–The Formative Years 1791-1841*. Baton Rouge: Louisiana State University Press, 1966.

Krist, Gary. *Empire of Sin: A Story of Sex, Jazz, Murder, and the Battle for Modern New Orleans*. New York: Crown Publishers, 2014.

Le Page Du Pratz, Antoine Simone. *The History of Louisiana*. Edited by Joseph G. Tregle, Jr. Baton Rouge: Louisiana State University Press, 1975.

Marquis, Donald. *In Search of Buddy Bolden, First Man of Jazz*. Baton Rouge: Louisiana State University Press, 1978.

Medley, Keith Weldon. *We as Freemen: Plessy v. Ferguson*. Gretna, LA: Pelican Publishing Company, 2003.

Rogers, Kim Lacy. *Righteous Lives: Narratives of the New Orleans Civil Rights Movement*. New York: New York University Press, 1993.

Rose, Al. *Storyville, New Orleans: Being an Authentic, Illustrated Account of the Notorious Red-Light District*. Tuscaloosa, AL: The University of Alabama Press, 1974.

Somers, Dale A. *The Rise of Sports in New Orleans 1850-1900*. Baton Rouge: Louisiana State University Press, 1972.

Smith, Norman R. *Footprints of Black Louisiana*. Xlibris Corporation, 2010.

Sublette, Ned. *The World that Made New Orleans: From Spanish Silver to Congo Square*. Chicago: Lawrence Hill Books, 2008.

Thompson, Shirley Elizabeth. *Exiles at Home: The Struggle to Become American in Creole New Orleans*. Cambridge, MA: Harvard University Press, 2009.

EXHIBITIONS

Permanent Collection, Le Musée de f.p.c. (free people of color), 2336 Esplanade Avenue, New Orleans, LA 70119, lemuseedefpc.com

"Purchased Lives: New Orleans and the Domestic Slave Trade, 1808-1865, March 17-July 18, 2015," The Historic New Orleans Collection, Williams Research Center, 410 Chartres Street, New Orleans, LA 70130

WEBSITES AND BLOGS

Brenda Marie Osbey, Black New Orleans Research Seminar, osbey.com/courses.html

CreoleGen--Creole History and Genealogy, creolegen.org

New Orleans Public Library, Louisiana Division/City Archives & Special Collections, nutrias.org/spec/speclist.htm

Trans-Atlantic Slave Trade Database, slavevoyages.org

INDEX

C